JAPAN
JOURNEY

JAPAN JOURNEY

The Columban Fathers in Nippon

Edward Fischer

Crossroad · New York

1984
The Crossroad Publishing Company
370 Lexington Avenue, New York, N.Y. 10017

Library of Congress Cataloging in Publication Data
Fischer, Edward.
Japan journey.
1. St. Columban's Foreign Mission Society—Japan—
History.   2. Missions—Japan.   3. Japan—Church
history—20th century.   I. Title.
BV3445.2.F57   1984   266'.252   84–14228
ISBN 0–8245–0656–1

JAPAN
JOURNEY

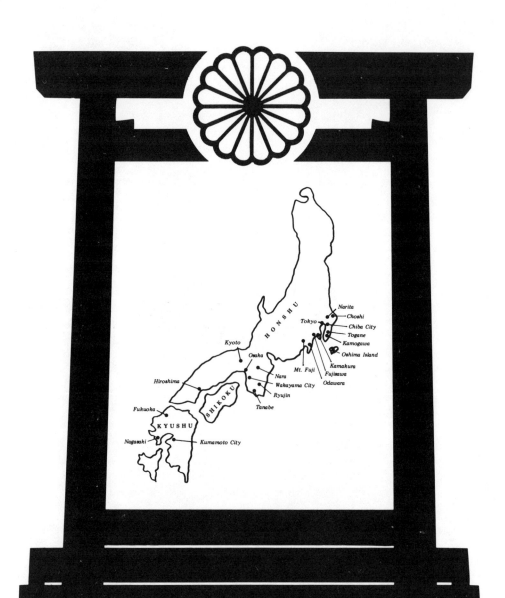

April 20, 1983
Wednesday

In the autumn of 1934, three young priests of the Society of St. Columban arrived at the Central Police Station in Tokyo to have their papers stamped for a trip to the interior. Fifty-odd years ago life was far simpler than it is today as evidenced by a poster on the station wall. There, translated into English, were the Rules of the Road.

1. At the rise of hand policeman stop rapidly.

2. Do not pass him or otherwise disrespect him.

3. When a passenger on foot heave in sight, tootie the horn trumpet at him. Melodious at first, but if he still obstacle your passage, tootie him with vigor. Express by word of mouth and warning, "hi, hi."

4. Beware of wandering horse that he shall not take fright as you pass by him. Do not explode the exhaust box at him. Go soothingly by.

5. Give big space to the festive dog that shall sport in the roadway.

6. Go smoothingly in the grease mud, as there lurks the skid demon.

7. Avoid tanglement of dog with your wheel spokes.

8. Press the braking of the foot as you roll round the corner to save collapse and tie up.

A half-century later I was on my way to Tokyo to try to find what had happened to the Columban missionaries and to write a book about them and the latter-day Japan. On the ten-hour flight from San Francisco, I sat next to a man, a Japanese, about my age. He was poised and elegant in a gray suit, a dark blue shirt, his black shoes highly polished. To use an old-fashioned expression, he seemed a "gentleman of breeding."

In the war he probably served the Emperor of Japan. Maybe, like me, he was in Burma in 1944. What if we had met in the Kachin Hills?

Fortunately for him a barrier of language separated us, or I might have bothered him with questions during the long flight across the Pacific. One thing we would have agreed on is that I am visiting his country on a mission that would have seemed highly improbable in the days of "festive dogs" and "wandering horses." Our paths never crossed again, but the picture of him, comfortable in Western dress, traveling the world as a matter of course, epitomized the changes I was to taste in Japan.

As I stepped through the door of the customs hall, a stocky man in a dark blue suit approached. With eyes on my hat he spoke my name. From his focus of attention I knew that this must be Father Kevin Flinn. When he had written to ask how he might recognize me in a crowded airport, I replied that I might be the only man on the plane wearing a hat.

With apprehension I approached this moment of meeting and surely he did too. We will be together every waking hour for the next few weeks, on a journey likely to have rough spots along the way. What if the chemistry is wrong? And yet at the instant of meeting I felt that we would get along just fine. Vibrations were good.

The agility and grace with which Father Flinn handled my baggage belie his sixty-three years. We had scarcely boarded the airport bus when we began exchanging family history.

His great grandparents emigrated, nearly a century ago, to Australia from Ireland. A kind of Irish handsomeness lights Kevin Flinn's expressive face, under wiry steel-gray hair. A twinkle suggests he is amused with the world as God created it.

Because of his thirty years as a missionary there, he was assigned to accompany me on a journey around Japan. I was to learn the story of the work of the Columban missionaries here—their inward and outward journeys.

As the bus rolled along superhighways, I recalled a Japanese writer having said that at night Tokyo resembles "a limitless sea of light," and, like ladies of a certain age, is fairest after dark.

This, the largest metropolis in the world, grew from ashes in less than forty years. It was a wasteland, a moonscape, after the bombings on the night of March 9, 1945. Only a few concrete structures stood. Incendiaries were most effective with old houses of wood frames, bamboo, paper walls, and thatched roofs. Nearly a hundred thousand people suffocated that night in the fire storm.

I brace myself each time I am confronted with Tokyo, a blend of hive and warren. Layer upon layer and wheels within wheels. No inch is spared. All is capped over, tunneled under, or traveled. Construction has devoured all available space. The tempo is fast, the energy high-voltage. Unlikely landmarks loom in the night: the castle of many turrets in super-sized Disneyland; the television tower, fifty-nine feet taller than the Eiffel Tower after which it is modeled, and a statue of Kentucky's Colonel Sanders much larger than life.

Tokyo's population is nearing twelve millions.

During the seventy-minute ride from Narita airport to the bus terminal, Father Flinn talked about how this Tokyo differs from the one that was here the day the first Columbans arrived. On October 20, 1934, two young priests from Ireland, Joseph O'Brien and James Doyle, reached Japan, and were followed later by Father Jerome Sweeney. They wrote home describing how buildings of Western architecture towered above those of Oriental design and Western dress contrasted with native garb, and cars competed with rickshaws.

Father Flinn said that the first three Columbans in Japan came less as missionaries than to learn the language. They were preparing to become pastors of Japanese churches in Korea, a country at that time ruled by the Japanese.

(When the Columban Fathers were founded as a mission society in Ireland in 1918, their entire focus was on China. In 1933, however, they sent eight priests to Korea; it was then they felt the need for a few Japanese-speaking missionaries.)

During the five years that the three Columbans stayed in Japan, learning language and customs, they served in various churches. In reports home they spoke with affection of their parishioners, an admirable people, educated and cultured.

In contrast to China and Korea, most Catholics in Japan lived in cities. The flow of converts was no more than a trickle. Even so everything connected with the Church was scrutinized as "a foreign influence," by a powerful group in Japan opposed to Christianity.

Conscious of this opposition, Japanese Catholics were not anxious to antagonize authorities. They remembered Japan's old persecutions, comparable to those of Nero.

When Fathers O'Brien, Doyle, and Sweeney were transferred from Japan to Korea things went well enough until the day of Pearl Harbor.

3

Father Doyle was under arrest for a time in the northern part of Korea. Father O'Brien, pastor of the Japanese church in Mokpo, spent a brief period in jail. Father Sweeney, because of his Australian passport, lived under house arrest for the duration of the war.

After the war, Fathers O'Brien and Doyle returned to Tokyo. When they arrived in January of 1948 they were appalled by the sight; eighty percent of the city was gone and the population had dropped from seven to four million. They stood in the ruins marveling at humanity's will to live.

Somehow life went on amid the rubble. Food was scarce, especially rice, the staple diet. Shops sold fish, vegetables, fruits, and bread at prices beyond the reach of most people.

Within a year there were thirty-two Columbans in Japan. One of the early arrivals, Father Kevin O'Mahoney, said that upon first sight of the country one was apt to wonder, "Will I be able to 'take it' here? Will I grow accustomed to the people, the language, the food, the climate? Time alone answered those questions."

The greatest lift to a young missionary's morale was to meet some of the old French priests who after spending forty years in Japan still loved it.

At the bus terminal Father Flinn and I transferred to a taxi for the long ride to the Columban House, in Kami-Yoga, a residential neighborhood in Setagaya Ward, in southwest Tokyo.

Gaudy neon lights flashed past us, surrealistic in their intense pinks and purples. Since I cannot read them they impress me with how frustrating life must be for an illiterate.

The first Columbans in Japan tended to learn the language as they went along. Since 1951, however, they have been taking intensive courses at the Franciscan language school in Tokyo. They usually take two years of study —in language, history, culture, and etiquette—and return a year or so later for further study if required or desired.

Japanese may be the most difficult language in the world for the western tongue to master. Reading and writing it are even more difficult than speaking it.

For the beginner, reading and writing are confined to the mastery of *Kana*, a purely Japanese script composed of ninety-six comparatively simple characters. Next comes *Kanji*, the difficult Chinese ideographs of which one must know a few thousand just to read a book or newspaper. The Chinese char-

4

acters number something like 40,000, but missionaries find they actually need only about 2,000 to get along.

Learning them through brutal memory, five or six a night, is a long hard journey. The student begins to wonder if it will be the next word, or the one after, that causes his breakdown.

Combining characters to form a new character is a real puzzle. Characters for "day" and "month" combine to signify "tomorrow." The word "darkness" is a combination of characters for "light" and "day" and "sound."

Counting is another matter! There are about twenty ways of counting, according to the different classes of things to be enumerated.

One of the most difficult things to learn is how to greet someone. The status of the person spoken to—superior, inferior, or equal—is acknowledged by the way you say, "How do you do?" Children growing up in Japan learn this in passing, but a stranger is uneasy dealing with such nuances.

The very atmosphere one creates while using words makes a great difference. There is *ma*, that pause which helps one say something while not saying it. And *enryo*, a diffident way of refusing something which really means one is willing to accept it. Then there is *haragei*, roughly translated as "belly talk" in which one communicates without words, only through artful silence.

Somewhere in Scripture it is written of the Jews that when they were carried into captivity in a foreign land: "They heard a language which they did not know." The fearful emotion held in that brief sentence is something a stranger in Japan feels every day.

While hurtling through the night, I wondered how taxi drivers ever memorize this city, for memorize it they must. Much of the metropolis is made up of villages clustered together with streets running at various angles connected by a web of alleyways. Few streets have names. Buildings are numbered by the date of construction rather than by position on the block. And since building crews and wrecking crews work all day and all night, things are constantly changing.

If a taxi driver fails to deliver you to your destination without difficulty he considers it a loss of face. I am told that when one driver failed to find the desired location, after assiduous searching, he pulled to the curb and buried his face in his hands.

Our driver tonight, without so much as a wrong turn, delivered us to the Columban Mission Central House. We entered the door where rows of straw slippers rest in solemn alignment. Of course not one pair was vast enough to house size thirteen feet, a problem I have in the Orient.

In the hall Father Michael Scully, a tall missionary from Cork, greeted us. With him were his staff, Fathers William Byrne, Noel Doyle, and Brian Vale and a couple of visiting priests.

This is the first time I have seen the new Columban residence, built four years ago. It has a good "feel" about it, a feeling that this is a good place to be, something every residence should have. I especially like the Japanese landscaping and the covered walks in the garden enclosed by a two-story red brick building.

Father Scully said that the Japanese architect was told, "This is the administration house for the Japanese region, but we do not want it to be like an institution. We want it to feel like a home."

The Japanese architect carried out his assignment well.

I asked if the cherry blossoms still shimmer this late in April. A few hold, but most are gone, somebody said. This must be the time of year of which the poet wrote:

> *Departing spring:*
> *with belated cherry blossoms*
> *shilly-shallying.*

The Japanese see cherry blossoms as a symbol of the brevity of life. They feel a sweet-sadness in all evanescence. A poet wrote long ago:

> *Ah, did you count the bell?*
> *Of the seven strokes*
> *that mark the dawn,*
> *six have sounded.*
> *The remaining one*
> *will be the last echo*
> *we shall hear in this life.*

Were a bell ringing now it would sound the stroke of midnight. This is a good time and place to end the first long day.

April 21
Thursday

The building trembled and a shiver ran through the furniture, "Earthquake," Father Flinn and Father Scully said in unison. "There may be an aftershock," Father Scully warned, but that did not come.

Such tremors happen about twice a month. Only newcomers like myself pay attention, especially if they are on the upper floor of a quivering building. Japanese houses are supposed to shudder but not collapse, because they have enough "give" built into them.

When the first Columbans arrived, in 1934, no structure in Tokyo was allowed to be higher than nine storys, a law that grew out of the terribly destructive quake of 1923 which started fires that burned 60,000 to death and was followed by a tidal wave that swallowed thousands more on the shores of Tokyo Bay.

"All of those tall buildings you see are supposed to be earthquake proof," said Father Flinn, "but the proof will come when we have a really big one."

Most mission work that is done by the Columban Fathers is in Chile, Peru, Fiji, Korea, Japan, the Philippines, Taiwan, and Pakistan. In the region of Japan, Father Michael Scully directs seventy-one priests, a few of them chaplains and teachers, but the greater number assigned to thirty-nine parishes entrusted to the Columbans.

One parish is in Tokyo. The rest are scattered through Chiba and Kanagawa prefectures, near Tokyo; through Wakayama prefecture, in the southern part of this island of Honshu; and through Fukuoka, Kumamoto, and Oita prefectures on the southern island of Kyushu.

In planning a journey that will cover that territory, we spent a good part of this morning. The day after tomorrow I will go with Father Flinn by air the thousand miles to Nagasaki, at the western end of the islands. We will work our way back by bus, train and boat through Kumamoto and Wakayama. After returning to Tokyo and catching our breath we hope to visit the prefectures of Chiba and Kanagawa.

A Columban from Australia, Father Leo Baker, went with Father Flinn and me this afternoon, to visit the only Columban parish in Tokyo, Saint Patrick's. The idea for its founding dates back to a September day in 1947 when Archbishop Doi of Tokyo spread a map on his table and studied it a long time. He said he was trying to visualize the returning families, the little shacks springing up in the bombed out areas and the highly populated places without churches. He pointed to a spot and said, "We need a parish there."

To begin a parish there, Fathers James Doyle and Joseph O'Brien returned to Tokyo in January 1948. What a cold, bleak place it was! They had no house of their own, but they had friends. The Franciscan Missionaries of Mary found temporary living quarters for them in their hospital and storage in the basement of the convent for their boxes and supplies, for no one was allowed to enter Japan in those days without bringing his own supplies.

A tiny stucco church went up on an odd-shaped piece of land surrounded by patches of barley and remnants of burned-out buildings. During the church's construction, an American car would sometimes slow down and a man in uniform, usually with wife and children, would look over the half-finished building with approving eye. Such families, from the army of occupation housed in an area called Grant Heights on the outskirts of Tokyo, helped in financing the construction. A military chaplain from Hartford and one from Boston were of great help.

On June 9, 1949, Cardinal Gilroy, Archbishop of Sydney, blessed Saint Patrick's Church. The Cardinal was in Japan serving as Papal Legate at celebrations marking the four hundredth anniversary of the arrival of Saint Francis Xavier.

At Christmas of 1949 the Catholic women's club of Grant Heights donated the Christmas crib to Saint Patrick's church; sent a cooked Christmas dinner to the priests, and to one Columban presented a cash donation with the frank instruction, "Please buy a new hat!"

There were twenty parishioners when Saint Patrick's opened its doors in 1949. There were twelve hundred when a larger Saint Patrick's was dedicated in June 1956.

Father Bede Cleary, the pastor of Saint Patrick's, said as we had dinner together that upon returning to Ireland after seven years in Japan, everyone he met asked, "What is it like?"

He repeated the answer so often that he felt like a recording. What his friends at home heard went something like this:

"I found that I do not have to sit on the floor, nor eat raw fish with chopsticks unless I want to. Every food we know in the West is sold even in the smallest town in Japan.

"I was surprised to discover—it was naive of me—that the Japanese are not all as yellow-skinned as daffodils. They do not all look alike, nor are they all rather short. They can be good-looking or plain, or plain ugly, even as the rest of us.

"Nearly all of them are black-haired.

"People dress well. Kimonos? No. They prefer Western clothes like our own. Colorful kimonos are reserved for weddings, feasts and some evening wear.

"The Japanese for the most part are courteous. I remember a man going several miles out of his way when I got lost on an early trip to Tokyo. I have had my bicycle mended by strangers on remote country roads. I have been served tea in a Buddhist temple. No one has overcharged me. The conductors on the buses say 'thank you' to each passenger individually. Clerks say 'welcome' as you enter a shop and 'thank you' when you leave.

"At the end of a baseball game I have seen both teams come to the center of the field, form two lines, and bow to each other.

"It is hot in summer and snow falls in winter and in some places it gets down to zero."

On the subway tonight I noticed a colorful poster above the heads of the people across the aisle. It showed five American girls, one playing a guitar and four gathered around singing. It was an advertisement for the YBU Language School.

By coincidence, Father Leo Baker, director of the school, was sitting next to me. He explained that YBU comes from *Yoki Bokusha Undo*, which translates to the Good Shepherd Movement, which was founded in 1952 by Father James Hyatt, a Maryknoll missionary. There are four such language schools in Japan, he said, and they teach about twelve hundred each year.

The American women who teach English in the schools are volunteers on a one-year assignment. They have responded to advertisements in Catholic papers in the United States. Each year a priest goes to the States to interview those who have expressed an interest. He usually has places for twenty volunteers, most of them recent graduates of Catholic colleges, although some have been working at a job for a few years.

After a month's training in Kyoto the volunteers are assigned to teach conversational English to students who have had several years of English classes in high school. English, required in all schools, is started in the fourth grade. Although university graduates have studied it for twelve years, most can neither read an English language newspaper with ease nor give helpful instructions to a tourist. That is because English is taught as a written language and conversation is rarely attempted.

Most teachers of English are Japanese and they are often not well qualified. University graduates who are adept in English are snatched up by big companies in Tokyo at salaries much higher than schools pay.

Since mission schools usually have foreign teachers, their students tend to take top honors in the annual English-speaking contests. That is why Father Baker's school is popular.

Japan's pride was hurt when told that among the peoples of Asia the Japanese are weakest in spoken English. This happened when the Asian Development Bank was being organized. The Japanese took for granted that its headquarters would be in Tokyo, after all that very name means Capital of the East, and besides Tokyo is the world's largest city and even the Olympic Games have been held there. Yet when the foreign ministers of Asia met they chose Manila as the headquarters for the bank, explaining that the ability of the population to speak English was a deciding factor.

The Japanese are making great efforts to remedy this deficiency because they must live by foreign trade. The private citizen wants to learn English because he has become the world's greatest tourist. Fluency in English may also mean promotion within his company or a chance to study abroad.

Being able to speak English has become a status symbol. Japanese sprinkle their conversation with English words, using especially the terms of sport and the names of Western food and clothing.

The profit made by the Good Shepherd Movement's language schools goes toward financing a nationwide apostolate of radio and television programs, though the schools raise only a small percentage of the million dollars needed each year. The rest comes from contributions by Catholics in Japan and in the United States, and other Western countries, and from funding agencies such as Propaganda Fidei, and occasionally from funding organizations for special projects. Father Leo Baker visits parishes in Tokyo and Yokohama to ask for contributions to help support radio and television broadcasts. He realizes that only broadcasting can reach most of the one hundred and twenty million Japanese. That is why he gives his time to helping the Good Shepherd Movement, sponsors of radio and television programs.

In 1957, "Light of the Heart" was started on one radio station; today it is broadcast over thirty radio stations. A television program of the same name, started in 1960, is now used by thirty television stations nationwide.

In the beginning program directors had to be convinced that a religious program would not lose listeners. However, the daily radio audience is estimated at over ten million and the television audience at about five million people.

A typical program might be about abortion. An advocate of abortion, Mrs. Kino, a woman doctor, discusses the problem with Shusako Endo, a Catholic layman who is one of Japan's most admired novelists, and Mr. Yamamoto, a literary critic. At the end of the program the audience is left with clear information about the Catholic church's teaching on the subject.

What are the results?

"One always looks for them, I suppose," said Father Baker. "The real results will never be known, for the workings of God's grace are invisible. The only measurable thing is that more than a hundred letters arrive daily at the Kyoto headquarters of the Good Shepherd Movement expressing thanks and appreciation and asking for further information."

Missionaries find the need to communicate in many ways, some of them unusual. One day Father Brian Gallagher was enjoying the cherry blossoms in Shinjuku Gardens in Tokyo when he saw forty teen-age boys and girls picnicking under the cherry trees. What drew his attention was that they were strangely quiet. He noticed their gestures and miming and knew the reason for their silence.

The Columban's interest in the deaf and dumb goes back to the time he mastered their sign language in Ireland. Hoping to recognize some of the Japanese signs he watched the group for a while. When a few seemed familiar he spelled out a greeting in Japanese Romaji. His first attempt was a failure. He tried again, this time more slowly and deliberately. Another failure. Then someone produced a piece of paper and a pencil and Father Gallagher's written explanation did the trick. Impressed by the tall priest's eagerness to communicate with them the children drew him into the middle of their group and in no time they were on the best of terms.

The simplicity of the Western alphabet took the children's fancy. Since the Japanese language has no alphabet, deaf mutes have to memorize some two thousand hand, arm, and body movements corresponding to everyday Japanese expressions. Finger movement, so prominent in the conversation of mutes in the Western world, are noticeably absent among the Japanese.

Father Gallagher was impressed with the intelligence of the children. "What one missed in our exchange of ideas another would pick up like a shot and pass it on to his companions." He told them of his family back in Donegal and of a mute Irish friend from whom he had learned the language, and of his work in Japan. They told him about school and of their plans after leaving school. They asked him to visit them and promised to teach him the Japanese sign language.

April 22
Friday

At breakfast here in Columban House I met Father Frank Carroll, of Dorchester, Massachusetts. His is the kind of mission that causes me to stand in awe; I admire the courage of someone who cuts himself off from his own culture to live within one wholly foreign.

When Father Carroll arrived on Oshima Island, seventy-five miles south of Tokyo, he found that his parish covered several islands, stretching hundreds of miles out to sea. Only ten Catholics lived on Oshima, where his presbytery was located. Another twenty-six were scattered over other islands.

"How did I ever get to be in a place like this?" was his first reaction.

Prisoners and political exiles were sent to those islands for centuries. The most famous exile was Julia Otawa, a Korean princess and the wife of a Japanese lord. She was exiled to Oshima in the sixteenth century because she had become a Catholic. During the first week of May, Catholics come each year from Japan and Korea to visit Julia's grave.

Most of the islands are old volcanoes rising out of the sea. The volcano at Oshima is still thought to be semiactive. It belched smoke and ash and turned the sky red at night until six years ago when an earthquake caused the inside to collapse and since then it has seemed dormant.

"Life on the island differs from that on the mainland," said Father Carroll, conscious of his understatement. "It is quieter and more peaceful. A traffic jam amounts to about three cars. The air is clean and free from pollution and the scenery is still as nature meant it to be.

"As a stranger, I wondered what to do with myself. How make a start? I visited a few Catholics on Oshima Island, but that didn't take long. I bought a little motorbike and later a small Daihatsu van and began exploring the

13

place. This was easy; there is just one road around the island connecting the few fishing villages. A few short branch roads run partway up the mountain. The rest is just empty mountainside."

The islanders, mainly descendants of prisoners and exiles, understandably tend to hold strangers at a distance. Certainly they do not open up when first approached. When Father Carroll went to the town office to register he had to ask help from five people before he found one willing to serve a foreigner. This startled him, for he had grown accustomed to Japanese courtesy on the mainland.

In June 1981, two months after becoming pastor of Oshima, he and Father Michael Molloy, the former regional director in Japan, took a trip to one of the most distant islands in the parish. They boarded the *Ogasawara Maru* which takes thirty hours to reach Chichijima, seven hundred miles away.

The population of Chichijima is twelve hundred with nine Catholics, all members of an extended family, the Kagawas. Mass was an emotional occasion. There were tears of joy tinged with sadness. Only God knows when a priest will come again.

The young Kagawas took the Columbans on a night tour to show them "green peppe," phosphorescent mushrooms that glow like jewels in the undergrowth. What the priests remember best about the tour is the "crunch crunch" as they stepped on giant African snails, pests brought from Shanghai years ago in the belief that if roasted and ground the resulting paste would cure tuberculosis. The snail now chews greedily on vegetation and has not provided a cure for anything.

The Columbans were hesitant to leave; the Kagawas and the other islanders had won their hearts. So had the beauty of the place with its bougainvillaea and hibiscus on every street, the gleaming white beaches that are excellent for swimming even if sharks bask close in shore, and the varicolored fish in waters so clear that fishermen can see them bite.

Back on Oshima Island, Father Carroll continued to visit his neighbors: "I found that among my nearest neighbors were five old ladies who each lived alone in a separate house. They were kind and returned my visit, each bringing a present. Soon when I was working, painting the house or clearing weeds from the garden, the phone would ring. Maybe it was an old lady asking that I go shopping for her, or another asking that I come and chase a snake from her garden, or one wanting me to carry a parcel to the post office. That is all part, I suppose, of being a good neighbor.

"I found that the best way to meet people was to go fishing. So I bought

14

some equipment and joined the locals where the ferry boat comes in. The first time all I caught was the line of the fellow next to me. Later I caught half a rowboat that was being taken out by the tide. I improved but though I did not catch many fish, I did get to know a few of the people."

Father Carroll is in Tokyo on his way to the United States. A Columban gets six months of home leave after each four years abroad.

When I look over a tightly packed crowd I wonder if I am the only person in the world over twenty. Tokyo seems a city of students. Especially high-school students. They stand out because of their uniforms—boys in their military cut black and girls in dark blue skirts with dark blue jackets or sailor blouses. For the most part they seem well behaved.

They don't look as worried as I am told they are when facing *shiken-jigoku*, examination hell. They take exams seriously from kindergarten to the university. The man who said, "The entrance exam for kindergarten may well determine the direction life will take," was hardly joking.

It goes this way: to get a good job one needs to be the graduate of a good university. To get into a good university one needs to be from a good high school. And so on down the line.

At exam time, in the spring, a gloom settles over the land. The pressure is felt from granny down to the youngest child.

At the university level the exam is called "the narrow gate." Through the narrow gate students enter Japan's 270 universities and colleges. Tokyo University, called *Todai*, shines like the sun in the solar system. A graduate from there has a prestige that nothing else can give. One commencement speaker told the graduating class, "You are the elite of the land."

Forty percent of students taking entrance exams fail to get into a university. There are about a quarter million such failures in Japan today; they are known as *ronin*, which means something like "wanderers." They have suffered the trauma of failure and face another year of study at home or in special "cram" schools. With next year's high-school graduates they will make another assault in spring on the narrow gate. Some few give up after one failure; some try as many as four times and finally succeed.

Mental breakdowns are not unusual even before the exams begin. Those who fail need courage to carry on, and those that lack the courage sometimes leave a note that goes: "I failed Mom and Dad. I disgraced my family. I caused a lot of trouble. I'm sorry." They have come to prefer death to life.

Even those who pass the test do not escape unscarred. Special clinics are set

15

up at the universities to help emotionally disturbed students. *Todai* university is hardest hit of all. Five percent of its freshmen suffer schizophrenia.

Akio Morita took a stand against this national intensity in a book, *Never Mind School Records*. Morita, the man behind the Sony empire, is a graduate of Osaka Imperial University. The theme of his best seller was that what really counts is talent, not the prestige of the school. Although the book caused comment throughout Japan two decades ago, examination hell continues as a national trauma.

Despite all of this, Japanese students love school. They would cry if the school burned down. Vacation time is boring and they count the days until school starts.

"Often a student loafs through university feeling he 'has it made', but not after he gets a job in a large, respectable company," said Father Flinn. "Diligence is highly respected. He works for money, but not for that alone. He shops around looking for the kind of work he would like. Self-fulfillment through work is an ideal."

The Japanese do not readily change jobs. Once employed they are not looking around for higher pay, better working conditions, and more fringe benefits. Each worker feels he has joined a team and is expected to put the welfare of the team above his own. The "father" firm guarantees a lifelong job and many benefits, if he stays loyal. This family feeling leads to a close relationship among fellow workers and such closeness makes changing jobs painful. Better pay or a more congenial atmosphere do not compensate for the lonely feeling of having deserted a benevolent family.

Work is not considered a necessary evil, something one does to get money for play. Leisure is seen as something that refreshes one for work. Weekends are time for recovery. The six-day week, with long hours, is usual in Japan.

"The Japanese is kind and friendly to intimates," said Father Flinn, "but shy and even indifferent to strangers. He is afraid of getting involved with people he has not known for a long time, or who do not work in his firm. Almost all his life is taken up with his place of work and all sorts of more-or-less compulsory organizations. He is always busy—in fact, too busy."

On the subway I observed that many high-school students are quite tall. Father Flinn remarked that he became aware of that the day the local school donated some old desks to his kindergarten. When they were delivered he noticed that wood blocks had been attached to make them two inches higher. Later he read that a seventeen-year-old boy today is four inches taller than a boy that age a half century ago.

Better posture and better diet seem to have added the inches.

As for posture, years ago desks were built low on purpose so that the pupil slumped forward, leaning toward the teacher in an attentive position, but now the "honorable bow" has given way to upright straight backs. For another thing, young people are not sitting on floors with their legs tucked under them as much as they once did. This position retarded proper bone development in the legs.

A change in diet did most to add inches to the national height. The Japanese eat nine times as much dairy produce, six times as many eggs, and four times the amount of meat they did before the Second World War.

What about rice?

"It is still forty-five percent of the Japanese diet," said Father Flinn. "But the consumption of Western-style food, especially among students and white-collar workers, has caused hundreds of rice dealers to close in recent years."

I came across the statistic that every thirty minutes someone in Japan commits suicide and for every one who succeeds seven fail. A Columban said he believes the Japanese are less fascinated now than they once were by the act of self-destruction.

During the Second World War the ideal was to die for the Emperor. Newspapers in Tokyo praised the young lieutenant who fell on his sword to atone for a slip of the tongue when reading an Imperial Edict. They also commended old General Nishiyama for committing suicide so that his pension might be used for the war effort. Kamikaze pilots, chosen for suicide missions, were national heroes.

Father Flinn said that although the deed may have lost its popularity the threat of suicide still crops up in unusual circumstances. He told of his friend, Mr. Isemoto, whose mother objected when he was about to become a Christian.

"This is an insult to your ancestors!" she said. "You should commit suicide. If you don't, I will."

The young man pleaded with her to put off the deed. "I'll commit suicide in four years," he said, "if by then you fail to see I have done what is best for me."

His mother consented to bide her time. In less than four years she became a Christian.

Suicide has become exceptionally banal now that it is used as a way of eluding loan sharks. During the first four months of 1983, in the face of debts, 409 persons killed themselves, nearly half of last year's twelve-month total.

Sometimes the suicide turns into group deaths. A man in Yamagata Prefecture, unable to repay the two million yen he had borrowed from a loan shark, killed his two children and himself by running exhaust fumes into his car through a hose. A family of four in Toyama Prefecture plunged into the sea in a car to escape a ten million yen debt. In Hyogo Prefecture a man strangled the wife of a friend and drowned her son in the river to get their health insurance certificates which he used as collateral to borrow a million yen from a loan shark.

All of this makes General Nishiyama and the Kamikaze pilots seem noble in comparison.

Juvenile delinquency is a dark cloud forming on the horizon. At least that is what I sense after reading a story in today's newspaper that quotes principals from 173 junior high schools. They complain that delinquent students tell lies without feeling guilty, are apathetic toward school work, and readily shift responsibility to someone else.

The news report continued: "More than thirty percent of the respondents said that a student's misbehavior usually starts with 'trendy' hairstyles such as perms, unusually long hair, and dyed hair, and advances to more serious misconduct."

This is in contrast to a report of several years ago when the government introduced a course in ethics into the high school curriculum. Students in the course were asked to pick the personage in history to whom they felt most attracted.

The greatest number wrote down Jesus Christ. Next in order came Socrates, Marx, Kant, and so on.

In answering the question about what religion appealed to them, the students preferred Christianity over their own Buddhism and Shintoism.

The startling thing about this is that these were public school students. One in five hundred might be Christian and one in a thousand Catholic.

When walking through a shopping arcade I find that the music sounds like that heard back home. Perhaps music has done more than anything to blend cultures of East and West.

When a Columban went into a woodworker's shop in Japan he heard a

18

carpenter whistling, "Believe me, if all those endearing young charms."
The Japanese did not know the priest was from Ireland.

Months later in Killarney the priest came upon a young lad riding down
the road on a bicylce whistling *Hitori botchi no yoru*, one of the top ten in
Japan just then.

"What are those?" I asked, pointing to a display of them in a store window.

"*Han*," said Father Flinn. "Without a *han* in Japan you are nobody." A
han is a personal seal, the size of a small coin, usually of wood or horn. In
special cases it might be ivory, jade, porcelain, or iron. On the seal is engraved in Chinese characters the name of the owner in distinctive and varying styles.

The seal is stamped onto a sticky vermillion dye pad and then imprinted
wherever you choose to sign your name. When you go to the post office,
obtain a license for driving or marriage, receive parcels or registered letters,
you need a seal. Usually a *han* is registered at the city office which issues a
certificate saying that this seal is recognized as belonging to you.

"Were there no *han*, life in Japan would come to a standstill," said Father
Flinn.

At frequent intervals vans drive past with loudspeakers mounted on top.
Women, evidently selected for their penetrating voices, turn up the volume
to do some electronic electioneering.

I wondered if I find the high decibels jarring because I cannot understand
what the keen-edged voices are saying, but then others must also flinch at
the sound, judging from an editorial in this morning's paper which begins:
"Election campaign cars just scream out the names of candidates. Drumming
names into voters' ears in this cheap way will end tomorrow."

Tomorrow we will be traveling and so maybe we will elude some of the
final horror. To travel while still under the influence of jet lag will be enough.

Although Father Flinn is only five years younger than I, he moves with
an alacrity that I cannot emulate. Maybe he will slow down on the southern
island of Kyushu because tonight he said, "They used to say that when you
reach Kyushu throw away your watch and pick up a calendar."

19

April 23
Saturday

Father Flinn lacked his usual ebullience and was downright pensive during the monorail ride to the airport and during the two-hour flight to Nagasaki. My first thought was that he might be making a spiritual transition from the hectic island of Honshu to the more tranquil one of Kyushu.

On the long bus ride from the airport into Nagasaki, I began to see that he was haunted by memories of November 2, 1947, the day he landed in Japan. He was remembering the scared young priest from Australia eager to begin a five-year appointment to the diocese of Nagasaki.

Then he saw the havoc! Homeless orphans haunted the streets. Many people were covered with keloids, the ugly sores that accompany radiation sickness. The slightest breeze still carried the smell of death.

Old people felt that "nothing can be done." The young ones refused to accept that. They sent the orphans to "blue sky schools," classes taught in open fields, and with the help of American soldiers dug a new life out of the rubble. They armed themselves with so much *kungiki*, fresh inspiration, that over all of that dead space they built a beautiful city.

Nagasaki has always been a remarkable place. Through the years it called itself Japan's "window to the world," because during the centuries of isolation this lovely port was a door kept slightly ajar. Through it came bits and pieces of the world's culture as merchants arrived and departed. Portuguese, Chinese, Dutch, English, and Russians left behind something of religion, architecture and cuisine. The Japanese have always had a talent for taking something they like, endowing it with their own spirit, and arriving at something charming.

The first person Father Flinn took me to visit was Joseph Cardinal Asajiro Satowaki. We approached the episcopal residence up a long flight of steps on the slope of Oura hill. The nicely proportioned red brick house of two storys, with verandas stretching across the front of each, was built last century by the Paris Foreign Mission Society. Father Flinn pointed to a window, on the left-hand side of the second floor, and said that he had lived there many years ago.

In the formal parlor the young Japanese priest who greeted us said the cardinal is ill and gave little hope of our getting to see him. Father Flinn handed the priest a gift for His Eminence, a bottle of brandy, asking that it be delivered. When the cardinal heard that his friend from Australia was in the house he had us brought upstairs.

As we mounted the stairway, Father Flinn said, "Time passes us all by!" He must have felt a surge of remembrance of the days the cardinal was in his prime.

Down the long stretch of red carpet we hurried to the reception room. From the way the prelate and the Columban greeted each other it was evident that their friendship goes back to the days when hardships brought colleagues close together.

The old man's jet hair, firm face, high cheekbones and especially the lively eyes all tend to mislead. They suggest that he is a decade younger than his seventy-nine years, until he walks, and then the shuffle shows. When I was introduced as a professor from the University of Notre Dame, the cardinal grew solemn and made a statement. I waited for the translation.

"The cardinal has observed," said Father Flinn, "that of late Notre Dame has not done well in football."

When the three of us settled at a low table a nun brought strong coffee and slices of sponge cake made from a recipe that arrived from Portugal three hundred years ago.

At this table, on February 26, 1981, the cardinal entertained Pope John Paul II. When the elderly prelate asked the Pope if he would go to the church next door to say a few words to an assembly of nuns, the monsignor in charge of the itinerary objected, but the Pope went anyway.

"He spoke for twenty minutes!" said His Eminence with evident satisfaction.

The cardinal's current illness began at the time of the Pope's visit. There had been too much strain making preparations. To intensify it all, the snowfall and the temperatures during the visit were the worst Nagasaki had known in forty years.

In February the ailing prelate will be eighty, the time of retirement for cardinals. He feels he might even see eight-five, but doubts that he will achieve eighty-eight, an age especially honored by the Japanese.

Evidently trying to switch the conversation from the end of life to the beginning of it, Father Flinn asked the old man to tell me about the remarkable place of his birth. Joseph Asajiro Satowaki said that he was born February 1, 1904, in Shittsu, a small village in Nagasaki Prefecture. In the village live 1,261 Catholics in a total population of scarcely 2,000. From it have come more than a hundred nuns, thirty priests, and two cardinals, the other being Cardinal Taguchi, who died in Osaka in 1978.

Of the 450,000 Catholics in Japan, 72,000 are in the archdiocese of Nagasaki. The cardinal estimates that there are about 100,000 "old Christians" in the archdiocese, about half of whom refuse to accept the authority of the Roman Catholic Church.

Old Christians are descendants of the Christians who kept the faith during more than two hundred years of persecutions which began in about 1614. Those who have not yet returned to the Church are known as *banare*, the separate ones.

The *banare* derive their religion from the time of Saint Francis Xavier. The story of their separation begins early in the seventeenth century when at the threat of persecution missionaries prepared their people to go underground.

The underground Christians divided their flocks into cells. Over each they placed four *ojiisan* (elders) and a *mizu-kata* (water man) whose duty it was to baptize the children.

When missionaries were allowed to return to Japan, in the middle of the last century, many of the ancient Christians refused to accept the French priests.

Whether or not they can still be called Christians is a question, for their ritual practices and their beliefs have become distorted through the years. Their Latin, for instance, is so corrupt that it is no more than senseless sounds and their belief no longer includes the immortality of the soul.

One of their saddest practices today is that of the *chago*. *Cha* means tea and *go* means assembly. Each month the *banare* meet with the ostensible purpose of drinking tea, but really to offer prayers in common. The prayer forms have suffered in translation, being handed down from generation to generation, so that now they are unintelligible.

If a stranger enters while a *chago* is in progress, the prayers are suspended and the *banare* resume drinking tea and chatting. Such suspicion is a relic of the time of the persecutions when a stranger might be a member of the secret police.

Describing the Christians who are no longer separated from the church, the cardinal said, "In Nagasaki there is a traditional concern for the spiritual life. One that does not tolerate poor values."

He believes that the church thrives in his archdiocese because of the religious education the children get in the home where there is a deep sense of faith.

"It is a depth that forms only after several generations of Christianity," the cardinal said. "In many parts of Japan priests and sisters and bishops have an intellectual faith, but not enough of it in their hearts. They become Catholics as adults and so the deep grain is not there. The bishops of Nagoya, Yokohama, and Sendai were university students before they were Catholics. When the faith is new, strange ideas can form. For example, some bishops try to bring ancestor worship into the Catholic Church."

In the archdiocese of Nagasaki there are ninety priests and over a thousand nuns. Only one man in the archdiocese has left the priesthood since Vatican II. Vocations are fewer than they used to be; caused by easy living and small families, the cardinal said. The sisters seem to be recovering their vocations; one society has over eighty aspirants.

While Cardinal Satowaki is optimistic about Catholicism in his archdiocese he is less optimistic about its future in Japan. "There is too much shallow feeling in the realm of the spirit," he said. "Shinto and Buddhism lack depth. Even primitive religions in Africa admit a supreme being, but in Japan there is no such admission. The Japanese have caught up with the rest of the world in technology and in business, but in religion they are still primitive."

As Father Flinn and I started down the stairs, the cardinal's parting admonition to me was: "Write only for the honor and glory of God. Don't write to make the devil happy."

Paul Aijiro Yamaguchi, the archbishop who preceded Cardinal Satowaki, had a feeling for Nagasaki that was almost mystical.

While studying in Rome he found the sky exceedingly beautiful, but thought the sky over Nagasaki even more so. Breathtaking is what he called the port of Naples with Vesuvius reflected in the water, and he stood in awe of the Rocky Mountains, the Grand Canyon, and the blue lagoons, coral reefs, and graceful palms of the South Pacific.

"But the landscape of Nagasaki," he used to say, " is a blend of natural and artificial beauty; it is like a masterpiece painted by a great artist."

The city, sitting on a peninsula, is surrounded by sea, mountains, and tiny islands. A deep blue sky reflects in the clear waters of the port.

The archbishop liked to climb to Glover's Mansion, just behind his residence. Legend has it that here a Japanese girl looked out to sea waiting for an American Naval officer. This became the basis for a story, then a play, and finally Puccini's *Madama Butterfly*. From the mansion the harbor is clearly visible—there stretch the Mitsubishi shipyards, tankers rest at the piers, and passenger ships and fishing boats are busy entering and leaving the harbor.

"If you have time," the archbishop used to tell visitors, "climb down from Glover's Mansion and cross the harbor. Take a ropeway and go to the top of the hill called Inasayama. That is a grand observation platform. There you see Nagasaki from a different angle. It curls around the harbor and eats deep into the valleys between the mountains. And you'll see the rivers flowing into the port. In the distance, to the north is the placid Bay of Omura. To the east is the Sea of Amakusa. The Sea of Goto, to the southwest, comes into view on a fine day." "Here," Archbishop Yamaguchi used to say, "God did his best work."

Upon leaving the cardinal's residence Father Flinn and I climbed the last few steps to a charming Gothic church that stands as a monument to the optimism of French missionaries. For instance, when it was dedicated, February 19, 1865, not one Japanese attended the ceremony; the police had warned against it. Father Petitjean could not even speak to anyone without fear of getting that person into trouble, and so he kept to himself and the church remained locked.

Inside the church today we found a large crowd listening to a lecture. I took for granted that this was a group of Catholics, but Father Flinn said there was probably not a Catholic among them. Tourists were listening to the story of how Catholicism was reborn in Nagasaki inside this very church.

They heard how Father Petitjean hoped to find descendants of Christians who had died for their faith three hundred years earlier. His hopes were fulfilled beyond expectation a month after the lonely dedication of his church. On March 17, 1865 the French priest looked out the window of his house and saw a dozen people, men, women and children, standing before the locked door of the church. He was struck by their respectful demeanor which indicated that they were attracted there by more than curiosity. When he opened the church door the Japanese followed him inside. He approached the altar and knelt to pray. A middle-aged woman knelt beside him and asked, "Where is Santa Maria?"

He led her to the altar of Mary.

Over a period of time other questions were clarified: "Are you married?" and "Do you follow the Pope in Rome?"

Satisfied with the answers, some Japanese said, "All of us have the same heart as you."

The three questions she asked him had been handed down from generation to generation. These are the ones to ask, tradition said; these will help you know the real from the fraudulent.

Soon so many Japanese were coming to Oura church that Father Petitjean became alarmed fearing the police might interfere. So he and his parishioners began to meet very early or very late, or on days of bad weather, or at any time that the police might not be on the alert. Soon many more hidden Christians were discovered. A man who came from the Goto islands to see a doctor visited Oura church and told the French pastor that his ancestors had fled to the islands two hundred years earlier to escape persecution and that at least a thousand Christians were still living on the islands.

On the other side of Nagasaki, at Urakami, about thirteen hundred Christians soon contacted priests and an equal number were discovered in neighboring mountains. Four temporary "chapels" were started in Urakami when priests went in the night, for police were issuing secret orders that Japanese should not visit a priest.

As we came out the door of Oura church I asked Father Flinn if he was sure that those people inside, so attentive to the lecture, were not Catholic. "They are tourists," he assured me. "They are so attentive because the Japanese have good manners and are also interested in hearing about religion."

Father Flinn said that there are 850,000 Christians in this country, but if you take the word of the Japanese you would think there are three million Christians.

Why should anyone claim to be a Christian who has never made the effort to join any one of the 110 different churches and sects in Japan?

"The Japanese admire what they see in church institutions," said Father Flinn, "but they don't seem to be ready for a lasting commitment. They like our universities, high schools, and kindergartens. They admire what we do in hospitals, welfare institutes, homes for orphans, handicapped, and aged. They like our church-related centers for English studies, tea ceremony classes, flower arrangement classes.

"They even like to read the Bible as literature. If a Japanese enjoys reading it he might then refer to himself as a Christian. They admire Jesus Christ, at least as a man. They like to get married in a church, especially a Catholic church. Films, plays, and books with Christian stories attract them. The admiration is there and the interest too, but most Japanese are satisfied with a superficial contact.

"Japan's traditional religions, Shinto and Buddhism, have never had creeds or catechisms. It is religious feelings, not religious dogmas, that satisfy the Japanese. They say that religion is a state of mind. The important thing is that one be satisfied with the present mood."

A young Japanese priest used the cardinal's car to drive us to visit Maximilian Kolbe's print shop, attached to a Franciscan monastery at the outer edge of Nagasaki. The hill that stands between the monastery and the city saved the fragile shop from the atomic blast in 1945.

Kolbe, one of the most recent of canonized saints, came to Nagasaki at the urging of the cardinal. Joseph Satowaki was a young priest in Rome, before the Second World War, when he met a young Pole about to set out for China to start a magazine. Father Satowaki told of the warlords, and the bandits, and described China of that time as an impossible place. Why not try Japan?

So Kolbe came to Nagasaki and built a few wooden huts high up on a hill. Soon he set up a small hand press and began publishing a magazine.

Pope John Paul visited the rude room in which Father Kolbe used to work and well he might, for, as he said, the Franciscan friar inspired his own vocation to the priesthood. Twenty months after the Pope visited Nagasaki, he presided over the canonization of his fellow Pole in October of 1982.

After returning home from Japan, Father Kolbe began harboring Jewish refugees and speaking out against Nazism, and so was a marked man when Hitler invaded Poland in 1939.

In prison Kolbe shared his meager rations with others and spent time comforting them. Some survivors say that he inspired them to go on living.

In reprisal for the escape of one inmate, in July of 1941, the Commandant at Auschwitz arbitrarily selected ten men to be starved to death. When one of them, a Polish Jew, cried out for his wife and two children, Kolbe, then forty-seven, offered to take the man's place.

With prayers Father Kolbe consoled his fellow prisoners. After he had survived two weeks without food or water a prison guard killed him with an injection.

Among the 150,000 worshippers who attended the ceremony of canonization in Saint Peter's square was Francizek Gajowniczek, the man whose life the Franciscan Friar had saved. After the rite was completed the Pope came forward, embraced and kissed the eighty-one-year-old man who had wept silently through the service. Gajowniczek told the Pope: "I was never able to thank him, but we looked into each other's eyes before he was led away."

The cardinal made arrangements for us to stay where Pope John Paul had spent a night in February of 1980. The Catholic Center, a new building, is attractive in its simplicity and is operated with grace and charm. This is something of a hotel where conferences are held by groups coming from all over Japan.

How quiet it is tonight. Even though this is a large sprawling city it gives off a feeling of tranquility. A deep spiritual tradition has been absorbed by the very earth.

In Nagasaki talking about the atomic bomb was taboo for years. In time the citizens began to feel that they ought to remind the world that atomic war is unthinkable. Japanese from all walks of life—especially school children—contributed to a gigantic bronze Statue of Peace which was unveiled on the tenth anniversary of the bombing. The figure, thirty-two feet high, stands on a stone pedestal overlooking the city. Its benign face is neither Oriental nor Occidental.

This beautiful, tranquil seaport facing the East China Sea has not been turned into a tourist attraction. Nagasaki seems to want to forget what happened at 11:02 on the morning of August 9, 1945.

April 24
Sunday

We had only to cross the street to go from the Catholic Center to the cathedral at Urakami, that section of Nagasaki where the bomb had its most deadly effect. The new cathedral—its 8,883 parishioners make it the largest parish in Japan—stands on the site where the old one stood when known as the largest church in the Far East. It was so near the atomic blast that nothing remains except fragments of statues and pieces of architecture, some of which have been placed in the gardens around the new cathedral.

About a hundred yards down the hill from the cathedral, a black stone pillar, twenty-four feet tall, marks the epicenter of the atomic bomb explosion. I stood at Ground Zero and copied the statistics: 18,409 houses destroyed, 73,884 people killed, 74,909 injured.

At the foot of the pillar is a simple bouquet of chrysanthemums. Near at hand a piece of stone rail salvaged from a bridge rests close to part of wall and arch from the old Urakami cathedral.

It is awesome standing in this little park looking around and comparing what meets the eye today with photographs in the nearby museum. How the human spirit can rise above things!

One photograph taken on this spot, in August of 1945, shows rubble, small pieces of almost uniform size, stretching off to the mountains. Burned contorted bodies lie in the foreground. There is a closeup of a girl whose skin hangs in strips and the charred twisted body of a boy. In another photograph bodies are jumbled together against a stone wall, the victims were riding a streetcar. The most symbolic object in the exhibit is an old pendulum clock, charred and smashed, with its hands forever stopped at 11:02, the minute the bomb, meant for the shipyards three miles away, exploded here.

We walked up the Hill of the Martyrs to see the monument, the museum, and the shrine. They were here because of a chain of events that began, in 1597, when a Spanish sea captain, rescued off the coast of Shikoku, boasted that Christian missionaries were being used to soften up Japan for an invasion by Western powers. When the shogun of Kyoto heard this he had seven missionaries and seventeen of the flock arrested for being Christians. The next day each had the lobe of one ear severed, the mark of a criminal. After being paraded through the streets of Kyoto they were marched on to Osaka as a warning to other Christians.

Five days later they were formally condemned to be crucified in the southern Catholic stronghold of Nagasaki. Two more Catholics were taken into custody for helping the prisoners during the trip southward.

To travel the five hundred miles from Osaka to Nagasaki the captives walked for twenty-six days in the hard Japanese winter. On a hill called Tateyama they were tied to crosses, and an iron band was clamped around each throat. A sign beneath them read: "Condemned to death on the cross because they preached the forbidden Christian Law."

Three of the martyrs were boys—Thomas Kozaki 15, Louis Ibaraki 12, and Anthony 13. From their crosses the three sang Psalm 112: "Praise the Lord, you children," until each was pierced by a lance. The execution was ordered by Toyotomi Hideyoshi, sometimes called the Napoleon of Japan, a general of peasant birth, who was described by an historian as "scarcely sixty inches in height, with a face as wizened as a septuagenarian ape, with supple and sinewy frame so wiry that it never seemed to know fatigue."

The twenty-six martyrs were canonized in 1862 by Pope Pius IX.

The monument to the martyrs, fifty-one feet long and eighteen high, is of granite and bronze. The granite, a yellow-gray speckled with red, serves as a background for the statues. The artist, Angelico Y. Funakoshi, gave the twenty-six bronze statues each a personality of its own and grouped them to form a singing choir.

The names are known of some 650 Christians and their missionaries put to death on this hill.

Behind the monument, a little up the hill, is a museum, three stories of ferroconcrete. Inside is told the story of Japanese Christianity, beginning with August 15, 1549, the day Saint Francis Xavier landed not far from Nagasaki.

When Francis left two years later there were a few hundred Catholics in Japan. Before Christianity was outlawed, thirty-five years later, the Catholic community had grown to 200,000.

Bloody persecutions began in 1597 because the governing powers believed such formidable foreign influence must be destroyed. In 1622, in a single ritual execution, fifty-two Catholics were killed. A few years later, of the 37,000 slaughtered in a fortress during the Shimabara rebellion, most were Catholics.

Soldiers killed four Portuguese ambassadors, in 1640, when they refused to repudiate the Faith. The Portuguese government was warned: "While the sun warms the earth let no Christians be so bold as to venture into Japan. Let this be known to all men. Though it were the King of Spain in person, or the God of the Christians, or the Great Buddha himself, whosoever shall disobey this prohibition will pay for it with his head."

This closed Japan for two centuries. All of that time a price was on the head of foreign and native Christians, and each year every Japanese was required to trample on the cross. Missionaries attempting to enter Japan were imprisoned and put to death, a story told in powerful detail in *Silence*, by Shusaku Endo, one of Japan's most highly regarded novelists.

During those two centuries vague reports came out of Japan saying that Christianity had somehow survived. This proved to be true when the French and the Japanese made a treaty, in 1859, and missionaries were permitted into port cities to minister to foreign residents only.

When the hidden Christians made themselves known, a bloodless persecution broke out in 1897. In those days a courthouse and a prison stood on the site where now stands the Cathedral at Urakami. Here Catholics were tried and incarcerated before being sent into exile. About 3,500 passed through the Urakami court in 1870; of these 600 died of ill treatment and hunger. Five hundred apostatized under torture, but almost all asked to be readmitted into the Church upon returning to Nagasaki at the end of the period of persecution.

It ended because pressure was brought by foreign governments. When Prince Iwakura's delegates traveled in Europe and the United States, "seeking knowledge throughout the world," they were constantly asked, "Why does Japan persecute Christians?" Two of the ministers finally persuaded their Japanese government that it could not get terms for a treaty so long as the old edict lasted. That did it. Noticeboards that proclaimed, "The evil sect of Christians is forbidden" came down in 1889. Persecution ceased not for any spiritual reason but for the sake of better trade.

Artifacts are well displayed in the museum. One of the most valuable is a letter that Saint Francis Xavier wrote to the King of Portugal. There are pieces of silk with traces of martyrs' blood on them and metal plaques bearing faint images of Christ crucified, worn smooth by thousands of feet that trampled on them to assure authorities of a disdain for the Christian faith. A sketch shows one kind of torture reserved for those who refused to deny their faith: a man is being interrogated kneeling on a sharp piece of wood, as logs are stacked one by one onto his shoulders. When Christians trampled on the image of Christ they sometimes went home and scourged themselves with whips and some of those whips are also on display.

At the top of the hill—above the monument to the martyrs and the museum—stands the memorial church. The Spanish architect Antonio Gaudi gave the twin towers the feeling of tortured arms stretching heavenward instead of the usual serene steeples pointing.

Although the theme of martyrdom imbues the hill, it is still a tranquil place. It could have been a vulgar display, but it has been done with sensitivity and taste. Nagasaki seems to do everything with style.

A farmer, Ogura-san, gave a Columban missionary a sign that had been posted in his village three hundred years ago. No one can read it, the farmer said, for the characters are archaic. Father Charles Roddy took the antique sign with him on his next visit to Tokyo and asked a scholar to make a translation. It turned out to be the law demanding the persecution of Christians.

Here is how the translation runs:

> Christianity has been forbidden for years. It is requested, therefore, that any suspicious person discovered shall be reported. The reward will be as follows:
>
> For information against a priest, 500 pieces of silver.
>
> For information against catechists, 300 pieces of silver.
>
> For information against apostates (who retract their apostasy) 300 pieces of silver.
>
> For information against those who shelter Christians and against Christian families, 100 pieces of silver.
>
> Moreover, to those who inform against people who shelter Christians there shall be paid 500 pieces of silver, according to the property

confiscated from the accused. When the fact that Christians are being sheltered is disclosed by one not a member of the "group of five" every member of the group will be severely punished, beginning with the head of the group.

The above command is given May, the second year of the Tenna.

The scholars said that the second year of Tenna was 1682. Persecutions had begun almost a hundred years earlier. The "group of five" on the sign refers to the spy system used during the years of persecution. The whole nation was divided into groups of five persons. Each member of the group was held responsible for the other four. If a Christian were found in any group and had not been informed on by a member of his group, the other four members were punished with him. Punishments were often horrendous. Burning at the stake and beheading were sometimes considered too humane and so every conceivable form of torture was tried.

Takegoshu, a Japanese historian, estimated that 250,000 Christians were martyred or exiled during the 250 years of persecution.

Although it was off the beaten track, buses came past at frequent intervals. The tourists looked out the left side to get a glimpse of a charming house surrounded by flowers and greenery.

Father Flinn pointed to a corner room, a sort of sun-porch, and said, "I took Communion to him there many times. He was a great man."

Dr. Paul Takashi Nagai, a specialist in radiology, suffered from leukemia while engaged in atomic research during the war. His condition was greatly aggravated by radioactive waves from the explosion in Nagasaki.

His two children were in the country when the bomb exploded, but his wife was at home. While searching the rubble of his home he came across the charred remains of a body; the only way he could identify it as his wife's was a pair of rosary beads beside it. He told of the experience in a book, *The Chain of the Rosary.*

During the six years of his illness, Dr. Nagai continued to write. Father Flinn found him at it each morning with a tablet resting against his distended stomach. The story of his life, *The Bells of Nagaski,* has a title that refers to some church bells destroyed by the bomb. When made into a film it was very successful in Japan. His book, *Leaving These Two Children,* about Makoto and Kayano who would soon be orphans, has recently been released as a film, *Kono Ko Nokoshite.*

Despite his suffering Dr. Nagai opened a clinic for victims of radiation, and although he knew his days were numbered worked on his book, *Introduction to Atomic Diseases*. During his illness he kept a microscope beside him with which he studied the effects of radiation sickness on his own body. He instructed doctors to use his cadaver to study the effects of atomic disease. The money received from his books he gave to charity; when one was translated into English he directed the American publisher to use his royalties to provide a library for Nagasaki.

The Emperor of Japan paid a visit to the doctor's bedside. Pope Pius XII sent his blessing. Eva Peron, the wife of the President of Argentina, sent a plaque of a madonna. An association of medical doctors in Italy sent a statue of the virgin, but Dr. Nagai was dead before it arrived. He died Tuesday, May 1, 1951, at age forty-five.

After leaving Nagasaki by bus we crossed the Shimabara peninsula to Taira-machi, transferred to a ferryboat which took us over the Ariake Sea to Nagasu where we boarded a bus for the brief ride to Kumamoto City.

Upon reaching the Columban church, in the Tetori section of the city, we met Father Joseph O'Brien. He and Father James Doyle were the first Columbans in Japan, the ones who spent five years learning the language and then went to Korea to work in Japanese parishes just before the start of the Second World War. Father Doyle died a couple of years ago; Father O'Brien, well into his seventies, continues his work here and has become something of a legend.

Although it has been more than forty years, Father O'Brien remembers the night in Mokpo, Korea, when he was in the Columban rectory with Monsignor Owen MacPolin and Father Harold Henry listening to the radio, waiting for the evening news. Since the news was in Japanese, Father O'Brien always did the translations.

The announcer exploded onto the air in a frenzy. The voice grew more violent with each sentence. Father O'Brien was reluctant to begin, but at last he said, "They bombed Pearl Harbor."

"The United States fleet has been destroyed," the announcer shouted. "The American imperialists have committed untold crimes against the Japanese. . . . The imperialists have long interfered with the prosperity of the Far East."

As the voice ranted on, Father Henry said, "They will come for me soon; I am an American. They won't bother you two, you are Irish. They believe I am a spy."

"What makes you think so?" asked Father O'Brien.

"They've often asked me at which bank in the United States I deposit the money I get for spying for the government. I don't think those who ask that question believe it, but the higher-ups do."

"We'll stand by you," said Monsignor MacPolin.

At that moment there was a loud banging on the front door. It had to be loud for the sound to reach all the way to the second story and to the back of that substantial brick building. As Father Henry started down the stairs the newscast was coming to an end.

Several Korean policemen, led by a Japanese officer, burst into the house and pinned the young priest against the hallway wall. They shouted excitedly, "Where are the other priests?" He said they were upstairs and offered to go after them. The officer ordered him to stay where he was and sent three of the policemen to the second floor. The rest began to search the house. Soon three policemen were dispatched to the rectory of the church up the hill to arrest two other Columbans, Fathers Patrick Monaghan and Harry Gillen.

The five priests were marched down the steep hill, herded into the Mokpo police station and lined up in front of Chief Morinaga. The chief's speech, translated by a Korean, turned into a tirade. Again and again he returned to the theme that Americans had tried to destroy the Japanese and now they themselves must be destroyed.

Outside a crowd chanted for the death of all Americans. Mokpo was thirty percent Japanese and a good many of them had rushed to the police station to start a demonstration the minute the newscast ended.

"Most of us are Irish," said the monsignor.

"But they cannot tell you from Americans," said Chief Morinaga, nodding toward the yelling crowd.

"But we are neutral."

"Yes, you are neutral," admitted the chief, "but you are neutral on the wrong side."

The Columbans were herded into a cell, about six by nine feet. It was a tight fit for five large men and an oval wooden box that served as a toilet. Here they would remain for days until put into other prisons or under house arrest. .

"Strange to say, our being jailed was one of the best things that ever happened to the Columbans," said Father O'Brien. "The Japanese sent a trained investigator from Tokyo to spend a year looking into our activities in Korea. He wrote such a glowing report of the work we had done there that the

Columbans gained new status in both Korea and Japan. It made us more effective after the war.''

Father O'Brien still has shock in his voice when describing the defeated Japan that he returned to: "You could stand at Tokyo Station and see the sea! People came up out of the ground like gophers!''

At Mass this evening Father Patrick Sheehy came down from the sanctuary, walked the length of the church, and gave Communion to a man in the back pew. Later he told me that the parishioner is a leper, married to one of the nurses at the leprosarium, and that he is physically capable of walking up the aisle to receive Communion, but psychologically cannot bring himself to it. He senses that there is a feeling of revulsion against him.

Friends of lepers and their families, too, believing that the disease is a punishment from the gods and is highly contagious, won't allow patients to return home even after the leprosarium is willing to discharge them. Employers won't hire lepers, either, and so the victims tend to stay on at the settlement even when it is no longer necessary.

In 1952 the Columban Fathers built a chapel at Keifuen Leprosarium, fifteen miles from Kumamoto City. Father Bernard Forde said that ninety of the twelve hundred lepers there are Catholic. He so admires their wonderful spirit that his eyes lit up when he told me, "They are the most spiritual people I have ever met!''

At Keifuen, one of fourteen such settlements in Japan, many cases would have been less severe had they been caught early enough. The trouble is that early cases go into hiding, fearing to be cut off from relatives and friends, and by the time they are discovered it is often too late for a cure.

The congregation in the little church at Keifuen is afflicted in varying degrees. In most cases the disease was arrested in its early stages with a minimum of disfigurement. There are some contracted muscles resulting in hammer-toes and claw-hands. This is caused by an imbalance of calcium in the bloodstream; the bone is absorbed until fingers and toes grow shorter and eventually disappear. The most pitiful cases are the blind; they have lost not only sight but also eyes.

Despair is the affliction that a chaplain must help his parishioners fight against. Some try to escape through drugs and some resort to suicide.

A Columban said that he found opportunities to try to live the prayer of Saint Francis: "Where there is despair let me sow hope." Whenever he read the gospels telling of Christ's relations with lepers he would recall the Gaelic saying: "God is hardest on his own."

April 25
Monday

While walking around the neighborhood early this morning I noticed an attractive bookstore and information center at the church gate. I mentioned it at breakfast and learned that Fathers Frank Hunter and Patrick Diamond had planned and built the shop in 1956.

The church here in Tetori is in the heart of Kumamoto City with its population of half a million. The biggest department store in town, Tsuruya, just across the street, attracts thousands of shoppers daily, and hundreds of buses load and unload passengers at the church gate. Non-Christians used to say to the Columbans, "I'd like to call at the Catholic church, but I haven't the nerve to walk through the gate." So Fathers Diamond and Hunter built a bookstore right next to the gate, hoping it might serve as an introduction. It must have worked, for Tetori now has more than a thousand parishioners.

Besides the church in Tetori, the Columbans have two other parishes within Kumamoto City, at Shimasaki and at Kengun. The pastor of Kengun, Father James Norris, a New Zealander, drove us out to see his attractive church this afternoon.

Kengun—the name means "to build an army"—was connected with the Japanese army for years, and even today the Defense Corps has a training camp a mile from the church.

At the time the first church in Kengun was built, in 1952, the area was mainly paddy fields and bamboo groves; it was the vegetable garden of Kumamoto. By the time the parish celebrated its twenty-fifth anniversary,

36

January 16, 1978, what had been farmland was becoming the bedroom suburb of the city, with many high-rise apartments and homes.

Most of the parish's four hundred Catholics are new Christians, baptized since the end of the Second World War. They represent a cross-section of the community—doctors, teachers, small shopkeepers, factory workers, farmers, carpenters. No one is really wealthy or really poor. The parishioners make the parish so financially independent that there is no need of support from abroad.

The new church, a well-designed ferroconcrete structure, was built in 1970 at a cost over $100,000. The debt has recently been paid off.

Father Norris is a remarkable raconteur. One of his stories concerns his role as a matchmaker. It begins with a policeman pulling a Japanese woman and her little girl through the streets of Hitoyoshi when Father Norris was pastor there. The young woman and her child, both ragged and dirty, were on the verge of hysterics.

The policeman brought them to a convent and told the nuns that the woman had lost her husband and was trying to earn a few *yen* by getting the child to dance in the street, begging for coins.

Soon the girl felt at home among the orphans, and her mother, Takazawa, responded to the influence of the nuns and developed into a woman of character.

Father Norris remembers the day that a farmer, tall for a Japanese and solidly built, came to the rectory shyly. After a profound bow, the visitor made a short formal speech, evidently memorized.

"Many of his idioms were new to me," said Father Norris, "but I understood enough of what he was saying to gather that he was a Catholic from down towards Nagasaki. I offered him a cigarette and he began to unfold his story.

"He was a farmer from the island of Kuroshima, where he told me, nearly all of the two thousand inhabitants were Catholic. The parish priest, he assured me, was a very fine man indeed. He himself was a widower, his wife having died a year ago leaving him with three children for whom he was greatly concerned.

"Then as if feeling he had been too precipitate in his personal history, he digressed to discuss the rice crop. From the rice crop he returned to his original theme, his concern for his children. Eventually he mentioned the name of Takazawa. Having mentioned her name he grew silent and stared at the table."

37

The priest began to see the pieces of the jigsaw puzzle slowly fitting together.

"Would you like to meet Takazawa?" Father Norris asked.

"Yes, *Shimpu-sama.*"

"You have never met her before?"

"No, *Shimpu-sama.*"

"How do you know that you will care for her?"

"She is a Christian, *Shimpu-sama.*"

"Then you would like to marry her?"

"As soon as possible, *Shimpu-sama.* The harvest begins at the end of the month. I will need an extra hand."

Father Norris said that he burst out laughing and was immediately embarrassed at having done so. He told the farmer to wait in the rectory while he went across the street to talk with the Mother Superior.

Takazawa was summoned and told of the widower waiting across the street. She was surprised but readily consented to come to the rectory.

"I introduced them to each other," said Father Norris. "They bowed and sat down. The man explained his circumstances, then put the all-important question. The Japanese do not believe in wasting time."

Takazawa said she wanted to think it over. It did not take her long. The banns were published and the wedding day arrived. Father Norris celebrated the nuptial Mass. Immediately, the farmer and Takazawa and her daughter left for the Kuroshima island in time for the rice harvest. Not a minute had been wasted. The arrangements for the next marriage of which Father Norris told me dragged on and on.

"His circumlocutions were exasperating!" That is how Father Norris remembers a former parishioner, Aoki by name. The dapper little man contrasted with his wife, an Amazon if there ever was one.

"When he had a point to make which he felt should be put across discreetly," said Father Norris, "he could really beat about the bush. He left me feeling I had shared in a great secret, but five minutes later I would find myself wondering, 'What precisely did he tell me?'"

This happy gift of conveying nothing while leaving the hearer feeling he has been told all fitted admirably into Aoki's delicate job of *nakodo*, matchmaker. The *nakodo* acquaints his clients with the history and circumstance of another family, presents photographs of prospective spouses, and makes whatever private investigations are believed necessary. When both families feel satisfied about the proposed alliance, the matchmaker fixes a day for the *mi-ai,* a formal occasion when the boy and girl meet for the first time. After the meeting they may agree to "date" for two or three months. If, after that, they feel suited to each other, the families exchange gifts. The marriage is almost certain to follow, with the *nakodo* arranging date, place, and other details for the wedding.

To be definite about how all of this works, Father Norris gave a case history in which he and Aoki were involved. He changed the names, of course.

It began when Aoki came to the presbytery saying he needed to find a young woman for the Nemichi family, one of comfortable circumstances in a neighboring parish. He said that the future mother-in-law required that the girl be a Catholic, with a good education and of a height to match her prospective husband's more than six feet.

"I thought immediately of Miss Suzuki and Miss Fukamizu," recalls the Columban. "Aoki knew the former but couldn't recall Miss Fukamizu, a recent arrival in our parish. I described her and Aoki again consulted with Mrs. Nemichi and the two of them decided to come to our parish the following Sunday to see the girls for themselves.

"It was a bad day for it. Miss Suzuki happened to be at home in bed with a cold, and Miss Fukamizu, who normally lingered outside the church with her sister, made straight for home on this particular morning because she happened to be on her own. All I could do was to point out her retreating figure to Mr. Aoki and Mrs. Nemichi. She was, at any rate, tall."

Aoki, however, favored Miss Suzuki, an excellent girl who had already refused a number of suitors, but now at the age of twenty-six was in danger of being left on the shelf. He described the girl in such a way that Mrs. Nemichi suggested he go to the Suzuki family and explain the circumstances. The Suzukis listened, and gave the matchmaker a photo of their daughter along with records of her education, health, and so on.

Mrs. Nemichi turned down Miss Suzuki: she was too short, and not gone past high school and her photograph, said Mrs. Nemichi, revealed a stubborn personality. Besides, she had a long angular face, not a round one.

"A pity, I thought," said the Columban. "I knew Miss Suzuki rather well and had a high opinion of her character. But it was the Nemichis' affair, not mine.

"Mrs. Nemichi's visit to our church for Sunday Mass hadn't, however, been wasted. She had noticed a third girl that morning who had appealed to her—Miss Kamiya. Mrs. Nemichi asked Aoki to make enquires in this direction. Before he did so, however, he had another task to perform. He

39

visited the Suzuki family and told them that the Nemichi boy had turned their girl down. It was the truth, but not the whole truth. The boy turned her down because his mother was not satisfied. But Aoki thought it more tactful to put it that way."

Aoki next called on the Kamiyas. The daughter who had caught Mrs. Nemichi's eye was the only Catholic in the family. When the families exchanged documents they began to see possibilities of an alliance. The next thing was to arrange a date for the meeting but before it could come off Miss Kamiya, aged twenty-three, said she was still too young to marry.

"Whatever her real reason for not wanting to marry the Nemichi boy, this certainly was not it," said Father Norris. "It was all getting a little beyond me: acceptance and rejection without either parties or families coming together. But that is the way things are done here.

"I was plugging for Miss Fukamizu, aged twenty-seven. She was tall, well-educated and had a soft round face. Since I knew her family, Aoki decided I should take along the photo and records of the Nemichi boy. I did so, telling the parents to get in touch with the matchmaker if they were interested. They were. The young couple survived the *mi-ai* and after a short engagement were married. Don't tell me that marriages are made in heaven!"

When James Norris was working in a government office in New Zealand he bought a watch with the name of Sagara inscribed on the face. He wore the watch while a student of the Columban seminary and was still wearing it when appointed to Hitoyoshi, for centuries the site of the castle of the Sagara family, feudal lords of the district.

The warlord who built the castle knew how to choose a site. The fortress must have been almost impregnable standing on a hill in the middle of the town, skirted by the Kuma river in front and a belt of hills to the back. Unfortunately, about a century ago a fire destroyed it, but the massive sloping stone walls sweeping up from the river still stand, a silent witness of the feudal age. The hill is now a picnic ground. From the high castle ramparts you command a view of the town below.

Father Norris was not long in the town when he found evidence linking the Sagara family with the flourishing Japanese Christianity of nearly four hundred years ago. People told him that five or six Christian *toros* were still to be seen around Hitoyoshi. A *toro* is a stone lantern erected over a pillar of stone, usually found at the entrance to pagan temples.

Shortly after Francis Xavier landed in Japan a Christian lord, Furuta

Oribe, designed a *toro* which would embody some Christian symbols. On the upright stone pillar he carved a madonna, and shaped the head of the pillar into a cross. These *toros* were sent to several Christian communities and a few found their way into the homes of retainers of the Sagara clan.

Father Norris learned this from Mr. Nishi, a Buddhist gentleman, who had placed a Christian *toro* in his old-world Japanese garden. Mr. Nishi also said that the present Mr. Sagara, the last of the clan, owned a letter written by a priest to one of the Sagaras nearly four hundred years ago.

The Columban had the opportunity to meet Mr. Sagara on a sunny spring day while picnicking on the bank of the Kuma with some of his parishioners. Sloping back from the river lay a beautiful garden, to all appearances a park with walks running through it. Father Norris was strolling the grounds when some of the young people from his parish told him that they had met Mr. Sagara and that the old gentleman said that he wished the priest would have tea with him. Mr. Sagara's bungalow lay near at hand, among a stand of trees.

The priest found his host, a man in his seventies, mild and gentle in manner. He and his wife lived in the bungalow a little distance from a large building that resembled a hotel. It had been his former residence, the old man said, but he had been obliged to leave it what with the war and the resulting taxation he could not maintain the place in a becoming style.

Over tea and cakes Mr. Sagara seemed pleased to have a chance to recall the past. Father Norris asked about the letter. Yes, he had such a letter and dug it out from one of his numerous trunks. It was written in *kanji*, Japanese ideographs. The priest could not read it, and it was with difficulty that the old man made out the gist, for the style of writing has changed considerably during the past four centuries.

The letter was written about the year 1581 and came from the once flourishing Jesuit mission in Yatsushiro where a Columban was now in residence. The letter merely said that the priest would like to discuss a certain matter with Sagara and would go into it in some detail when they met.

Later Father Norris paid a visit to the cemetery of the Sagaras. Beginning with the first Sagara, over seven hundred years ago, the graves of all feudal lords and their families are carefully preserved in what is now a small park.

The missionary decided to visit the temple connected with the clan and to pay his respects to the Buddhist priest. While walking within the temple grounds he met a gardener working hard at a vegetable plot. When Father Norris said he would like to see the temple the gardener ushered him into a house; left him alone in a room, but returned shortly in a long graceful kimono, bowed profoundly and introduced himself as the priest and custodian of the temple. The Buddhist priest showed the Columban various statues, instruments and vessels used in worship, many of them centuries old. The temple's most treasured possessions were some relics of Buddha brought from India.

After showing Father Norris the sights, the Buddhist priest and his wife treated their visitor to tea and biscuits. When the subject of *toros* came up, the Buddhist said there was one within the temple grounds and had been for centuries.

The *toro* was lying among weeds and propped against a tree, with the lantern top missing. While apologizing for the state of it, the Buddhist said that many people had come to see it and some had even offered to buy it, but he would not sell because he had in mind to erect it properly himself.

"Would you consider selling it to the Church?" the Columban asked. "Catholics could best appreciate its true value and significance, and if it were erected on church grounds it would be well looked after and would still be in Hitoyoshi."

Father Norris' heart beat wildly while the Buddhist spent several long minutes debating with himself. Finally, he said he would not sell it but would give it to the Church. That very evening the missionary had the *toro* transported to the church grounds.

Flushed with this first victory, Father Norris went the following day to visit an old lady who also owned a *toro*. Standing by it in her garden, the priest used his best arguments in his best Japanese while asking her to sell it. She had the name of being an obstinate old lady and, as she hung her head on one side, purring in ominous manner, it was evident the going would be difficult. She would not give a final answer today, but would think it over and tell him the following week. True to her word she came to the church dressed in her best kimono. Her husband had died a Catholic, she said, and so she would give the *toro* to the Church if Father Norris would say a Mass once a year in memory of her husband.

That is how two ancient *toros* happened to adorn the entrance to the Catholic Church in Hitoyoshi.

From time to time Father Norris and the last of the Sagara family met for tea. The old man was a Buddhist, but like many of his countrymen knew little of Buddhist teaching. As he was along in years he was anxious to prepare for the next life but did not feel that Buddhism was the answer for him. He wanted to investigate Christianity.

The heavy taxes were much on Mr. Sagara's mind. Formerly he had been a wealthy man but of late he had been forced to sell most of his property to make ends meet. All that remained to him now was this small property of twenty acres, a house, and cottage. He did not want to sell what had been the summer residence of the family for over two hundred years.

Then one day he put an unexpected proposition to Father Norris. He had been talking the matter over with his wife and had come to this decision: if the Church were interested he would donate his remaining property to it, rather than sell it whole or break it up. The Church, he felt, would be able to make good use of it, and he would ask in return only some simple provision for his wife and himself for the few years that remained to them. He had decided, too, to study Christian teaching, for he felt that it might be for him the solution to the riddle of life. After all had not many of his ancestors been Christians?

Hitoyoshi appealed to Father Norris from the first moment he saw the clean little town locked up in the hills with a swift-flowing river running through the center. Perhaps it was the natural hot springs that attracted him most, for they reminded him of his home town, Rotorua, New Zealand, where he had natural hot water in the back yard.

The name Hitoyoshi means "good man" and Father Norris found the charming people living up to the name. He was not lonesome there even when he was the only priest in the district of 150,000 souls; the next nearest priest was at Yatsushiro, thirty miles away.

The fact that there was a Catholic mission in Hitoyoshi excited interest among the Buddhists. Many strange callers arrived at the rectory door.

One day a young man who wanted to end his life but could not find a suitable place to do it, happened to pass the church and, on sudden impulse, called in to talk it over with the priest. He wound up talking himself out of suicide.

On another day a policeman knocked at the door and inquired of the housekeeper, "Is God (*Tenshu*, Master of Heaven) at home? "The housekeeper, nonplussed, asked what he meant. It turned out he was looking for Father Norris.

While we talked of the work of missionaries in Japan, I said something about the people being materialistic. Father Norris disagreed with that characterization. If the Japanese are materialists, he said, they are not hardcore materialists. They have spiritual values. They may not be religious in the traditional sense of the word, but their concerns go beyond the material.

Their spiritual life is centered in aesthetics. Beauty and nature bring them satisfaction. They find spiritual outlet in celebrations, flower arrangement, the tea ceremony, the theater, lovely gardens, and hundreds of other things that reflect deep inner resources and sensibilities that rise above mere accumulation of material things.

"Where do your satisfactions lie?" I asked.

"To teach a highly intelligent people in their own language," said Father Norris, "that is a challenge that has its satisfactions. And has its hurts."

He described how it is to speak to his parishioners about the goodness of God, to feel satisfaction in it, and then have a reaction set in.

"After I get back to the quiet of the rectory, it dawns on me that there seemed to be absolutely no reaction. After thirty-five years in this country I should know that it is unreasonable to expect any immediate response. But even so there is always disappointment. A feeling of failure. Some heartache."

When such feelings move in, like dark clouds in the sky, Father Norris unburdens himself to Brother Sugiyama, who drives the kindergarten bus and does a thousand odd jobs around the church. Once more Brother Sugiyama explains that no missionary should expect too much too fast. Don't ever forget that the Japanese have a long history and culture completely different from the Christianized West. In the Japanese tradition there is no notion of a single, infinite Creator who loves man and looks for union with him.

"Don't expect Christianity to be accepted overnight," says the brother. "Look at Europe; it took centuries to permeate the culture."

Brother Sugiyama gets Father Norris to admit that the Holy Spirit usually does not do violence to nature. The Spirit respects the freedom of individuals and nature, allowing the natural interplay of forces and the upheavals of history to work slowly, ever so slowly. That is how it will probably be in Japan. It will take centuries.

At this point the brother makes the priest face up to some uncomfortable facts.

"Look at Europe and the West now. Has it kept the faith that is the basis of its culture? You admit that the Japanese often show higher morality and greater social justice. And there is a lower crime rate here than in many so-called Christian countries.

"We Japanese are pragmatic. We judge the value of things by physical results. We are not deep thinkers who can immediately appreciate the spiritual depths of the Christian religion. We take a good hard look at Christians and judge from what we see."

Our afternoon together came to a close with Father Norris admitting that he is too impatient. He finds it hard to face the fact that this is the seedtime, not the harvest.

April 26
Tuesday

This morning Father Flinn and I took a bus from Kumamoto City to Amakusa Island. Columban missionaries, assigned to three churches on the island minister to a thousand Christians. Father James Morahan serves 204 parishioners at Hondo, Father Vincent McNally, 480 at Ooe, and Father Patrick Diamond, 317 at Sakitsu.

When the great persecution began in 1614 this island was home for 30,000 Christians who supported forty-seven churches and two thriving seminaries.

A printing house, established here by Jesuits nearly four hundred years ago, published books of such quality that the work was known throughout the civilized world. On a Gutenberg press, using metal and wood type, the printers turned out dictionaries, books of religion, literature, and grammar. The twenty-nine books that survive are a handsome tribute to the Japanese who learned their craft so well when the Jesuits sent them to Portugal to study printing.

When Father Morahan built a small chapel here in 1951 he became Hondo's first pastor in 350 years.

Christianity reached these parts a scant nineteen years after Francis Xavier arrived in Japan. In 1568 the lord of Hondo invited missionaries from Nagasaki to work in his domain, the capital of Amakusa. His wife was annoyed with him for doing this. She, being a devout Buddhist and something of an amateur theologian, urged Buddhist priests to start an insurrection demanding that missionaries be banished. The overlord of the island, Otomo Yoshishige, sent troops to quell the uprising.

Soon the lord of Hondo was baptized. His wife, after a series of debates with missionaries, was also converted. Other rulers on the island followed the lead set by the lord of Hondo and before long Amakusa was a very Catholic island.

Then came the long persecutions and the church of Hondo disappeared.

Not many Christians live on Amakusa today and yet the government here promotes the history of Christianity as something of a tourist attraction. Shops display such shabby souvenirs as Amakusa maidens with rosaries around their necks and boxes of "Christian candy."

An intelligent taxi driver, who knows local history, drove us up a hill above Hondo. At the top we found a monument honoring those who died in the Amakusa-Shimabara rebellion and a new museum displaying artifacts from the early days of Christianity.

Near the museum stands a bronze statue of a sixteen-year old boy, Shiro Tokisada, a leader in the rebellion. The strange thing about the uprising is that Christians of the districts, Amakusa and Simabara, accepted persecution for years; it was not until the taxes became excessive that they joined non-Christians in an armed revolt.

Even in times of poor crops and famine the lords of Amakusa and Shimabara were inventing new taxes. They even established birth and death dues and taxes on hearth and door and window. Failure to pay meant torture or even death.

Many who failed to pay were wrapped in rice-straw coats called *mino* and set fire. The contortions of flaming victims came to be called the *mino* dance.

When the daughter of a village headman was publicly burned for failing to pay a tax, her father and several villagers killed the tax collector. At the same time a group of samurai, out of work because they were Christians decided to revolt against their rulers. They chose a sixteen-year-old boy, known now as Amakusa Shiro, and called him "a leader sent from heaven," feeling that this would unify the people and put some spirit into them.

It worked well enough to enable them to capture Hara castle in Shimabara in October of 1637. An army of 100,000 soldiers, led by the shogun's best generals, failed to retake the castle and suffered heavy losses.

After two months the Dutch, in the interest of better trade, decided to curry favor with the shogun, the military dictator, by sending a warship from their trading post in Hirado. For fifteen days they shelled the castle from far out at sea, beyond the range of the insurgents' guns.

The rebels surrendered, April 12, 1638, when food and ammunition were gone. Amakusa Shiro and thirty-seven thousand of his followers were slaughtered, among them fourteen thousand women and children.

The lords of the districts realized that this was a peasant revolt and each committed *hara-kiri* to atone for their defective administration. The Tokugawa government, however, did not want word to get around that there had been misrule in the land. So the government called the revolt a religious movement, Christian inspired. That is when the Christians went underground for more than two hundred years.

In the new museum on the hill we found artifacts similar to those in the museum on the Hill of the Martyrs in Nagasaki: wood notice boards offering rewards to anyone informing on Christians; statues of Kannon, the Buddhist goddess of mercy, holding a child in her arms, used by Christians to remember the Madonna; and well-worn bronze plates engraved with Christian symbols, which Japanese were required to trample on once a year to indicate a disdain for foreign religion.

The museum is well designed and the exhibits well presented. Fortunately, whoever planned the displays on the hill avoided following the trashy example set by the shops in Hondo.

Father Vincent McNally is pastor of Ooe, a village on the southwest side of the island, one that retains a bit of old Japan. The language of its people, now looked down upon as a peasant dialect, was the speech of knights four centuries ago.

The passage of time is counted in Ooe by a Chinese calendar two thousand years old. New Years' Day falls in the middle of February, at the start of spring, and the year continues on, out of step with the rest of the world, but in harmony with the seasons. The people of Ooe have tiny farms that cling to the sides of the hill or nestle in the valley running between the hills down to the sea.

Their homes have high thatched roofs unusual in Japan. A Japanese professor holds the theory that since Ooe was traditionally Christian the people may have adopted the architecture of the high sloping roof found in many Christian churches. The faith has been around Ooe, on and off, ever since the days of Francis Xavier.

As you walk out along the road from the harbor, past the school and the Buddhist temple, you see a grey church tower peeping over a grove of bamboo and pine trees. The ancient Japanese found it fitting to climb a hill to pray so many of the old shrines and temples are sitting atop hills. The French missionary may have had this in mind when he located this fine Romanesque church on a high place. After a laborious struggle up the narrow rocky path you turn a corner, and suddenly you're there. It is symbolic of the struggle through life to reach a reward at the end.

The atmosphere of a Shinto or Buddhist holy place mixed with that of an old European cathedral pervades the church at Ooe. There are no seats or kneelers, the entire floor is covered with *tatami* matting. Statues of Sts. Paul Miki and Louis Ibaragi, martyrs of Nagasaki, Our Lady of Lourdes, and St. Francis Xavier adorn the sanctuary. Four archangels, now the worse for wear, adorn the sacristy.

Thousands of tourists, who come to Amakusa island in summer, visit the church at Ooe. As many as a hundred at a time come perspiring up the hill in straw hats, white shirts, summer frocks, all laden with cameras. For most it is their first visit to a Catholic church.

They stop *en masse* to read a piece of verse inscribed on a stone by a famous poet who once visited the church and wrote his appreciation. A representative comes to the pastor's door, bows, and asks for permission to see the church. The visitors take off their shoes and file in.

A sharp sibilant intake of breath through a hundred sets of teeth is followed by *"Ho-hoooo, subarashii nee,"* the Japanese way of showing that one is being bowled over.

The less devout, having shrugged off any religious feeling, begin to smoke as they look around. The more devout make their way to the high altar and with hands joined near the forehead, fingers pointing upwards, bow stiffly to "Kamisama."

When Father Bede Cleary was pastor of Ooe he often served as guide to the visitors. On one occasion when he was ill, he asked a man who served as sacristan and cook to give a talk to the tourists. This able fellow had been appropriately nicknamed the Fac (for factotum) by Father Eamonn Dooley. A literal translation of his Japanese name was Mr. Mouth-of-the-River. And since he was so adept at making pancakes—he served them at every meal—a visiting Columban, Father Robert Conley, conferred on him the additional title of the Pancake King.

The day that Fac served as a guide to a large group of tourists one of them carried a portable tape recorder. Father Cleary had the good fortune to hear the tape later.

"Everyone sit down please," said Fac, or Mouth-of-the-River, or the Pancake King, whichever you prefer. "No, no everyone face that way— God is up behind that white veil. This church is as you see, built entirely of concrete."

There followed a brief summing up of Christian doctrine.

"Now, has anyone any questions?" asked Fac.

"The foreigner we saw over there, who is he?"

"He is a priest of this church. He is from a country called Ireland."

"Does his wife live here, too?"

"No, you see Catholic priests don't marry."

The recording captured a sibilant intake of breath.

"Who cooks for him then?"

"I do."

"What kind of food does he eat?"

"Butter, milk and so forth."

"How does he eat butter, milk, and so forth?"

Here the Pancake King took a deep breath and really got into his work: "Well, you see, you put milk in a bowl and mix in flour and sugar and an egg. Then you beat it like this. Then you fry it on a pan."

One reason we visited Amakusa island was to see some of rural Japan. Our travels so far had been to crowded places.

You need not travel long in this country to realize that not much of the land grows food. About six out of every seven acres are so mountainous that not even the Japanese can cultivate them. Level land is found only in river valleys and on the seashore. The state of Indiana has more acres under cultivation than does all of Japan. Here there are more than four thousand Japanese for each square mile of arable land, the highest ratio in the world.

So Japanese farmers use every scrap of earth. Abandoned roadways, triangles formed by the convergence of roads, and even spaces between the foundation stones of burned out houses are put to use in some way. From such intensive farming comes a variety of crops: wheat, barley, tobacco, vegetables of all kinds, mulberries for feeding silkworms, and rice. Over fifty percent of the arable land grows rice which provides more than food. Liquor comes from fermented rice. Cheap umbrellas are of rice paper. Hats are fashioned from rice straw. A mixture of rice straw and mud makes plaster.

The Japanese are so imaginative in the use of land that Burma and India asked them to come and teach methods of crop rotation. Sometimes two crops grow in the same field in the same year; often one crop is sown before its predecessor is harvested. Barley and wheat, for example, are usually planted in furrows; a few months before the grains ripen a farmer will sow a crop, such as tomatoes, between the furrows, so that when the grains are harvested the furrows can be split and the tomatoes are off to a good start.

Such intensive cultivation leaves little land to provide fodder for animals, and so livestock is scarce. Fortunately the Japanese have a great liking for fish found in abundance in the surrounding waters.

How the Japanese love rice! No plot of ground is too small to grow it, provided there is irrigation. Even the mountainsides are cut into tiny fields of terrace upon terrace, like a giant stairway. Each field is a few inches lower than the other and so water flows constantly over them.

"How to obtain water might baffle the best engineer," said Father Patrick Diamond, the pastor of Sakitsu near the south end of the island. "The labor involved in laying the water pipe might daunt the men who built the pyramids. But when the Japanese farmer wants to get water he gets it. Somehow! If no natural source of water comes from above, he builds reservoirs. They fill readily during the rainy season beginning in June."

Father Diamond recalls quarrels among farmers over waterways. If water becomes scarce woe betide the greedy farmer, with land above, who stops the flow to fields below. It was not uncommon for a farmer to wound or even kill a neighbor tampering with the lifeline of a rice crop. Such arguments are usually settled at the village level; if taken to the courts the time to settle might be so prolonged that several fields of rice would be lost.

No fences separate the fields in Japan. That would mean a waste of valuable land. Banks of earth about a foot high run between rice fields to ensure a sufficient level of water for the crop; often beans and peas grow atop these banks to hold the soil together and to take advantage of every bit of fertile earth. In the past thirty years concrete walls about four inches thick have begun replacing banks of earth.

"In such fields Japanese farmers spend much of their lives. The day begins at sunup and as evening falls you can see them coming home very weary," said Father Diamond. "They return to their little hamlets of thatched cottages which cluster where the rice fields end and the mountains begin."

The life of the farm woman is a little less difficult than it was when the Columbans arrived several decades ago. She still rises early, prepares breakfast, sends the children to school, helps feed the livestock, and then joins her husband in the fields. If she has a small child she brings it with her and places it under an umbrella at the side of the field or keeps it strapped to her back as she works. From time to time she pauses to feed it.

When the day in the field ends the mother returns home to face a thousand-and-one jobs before she can rest for the night. Sunday is the same as

Monday with no days off during the week. There is some free time at New Year and during August when the family visits a temple or shrine to pay respect to the souls of ancestors. There may be a village celebration at the beginning of rice planting or at the harvesting. Modern machinery and electrical appliances have eased the Japanese woman's toil somewhat.

When Father Fred Hanson was a pastor on Amakusa his neighbor planted a plot sixty by twenty-five yards just outside the rectory window; the missionary followed the crop each day from planting to harvest.

The manuring, ploughing and flooding began in July. This done by father and two sons. Next the mother and daughter transplanted the young six-inch rice shoots from a tight little water-logged bed some distance away. They accomplished this back-breaking job in one day, never straightening themselves except for the customary breaks for dinner and tea.

In early November the Japanese family harvested the crop. They cut every stalk with a little hand reaper, hung the stalks to dry for a few days on a bamboo trestle, threshed them with a little hand and foot machine, and sacked the result.

The farmer brought Father Hanson a sack of rice as a way of saying thanks for the role the missionary had played as scarecrow's assistant. The scarecrow consisted of tin cans, holding a handful of pebbles, fastened to bamboo poles which were linked together by a rice straw rope gaily decorated with multicolored rags. When a rope at one end of the field was pulled all the tin cans were set in motion at once. Each time Father Hanson passed the rope he gave it a few tugs.

Farmers are not so poor as they used to be when they threshed and winnowed the way farmers did in the Palestine of Christ. Now they own small but very efficient threshing and winnowing machinery. Electric motors drive these machines, for there is scarcely a place in Japan without electricity. There are also gasoline machines on caterpillar tracks called "self-propelled, rice planting, harvesting, threshing, and bagging machines."

Japanese agricultural students, in order to learn more efficient methods, used to go to America to study. There they were astounded at the amount of land owned by the average American farmer. In time they decided that no parallel could be drawn between the small farms of Japan and the vast ones of America and so now they go to Europe where farms are smaller.

Farm machinery is often purchased through the community with each farmer contributing according to the size of his field. Planting of rice is also a community project. Farmers plan together such matters as waterway construction and road and bridge repair. Anyone who violates the code of community may find himself the victim of *Mura-hachibu*, a boycott by other members of the community. It is relaxed only when the offenders suffers some serious trouble such as a fire or a death in the family. The boycott is not common in modern Japan and is not observed with the same rigor as it used to be.

And despite all the work of farming, floods and typhoons often ravage farmlands. When water subsides and wind eases the farmer goes back to the field with hope. His patience is summed up in the expression: *"Shikata ga nai."* "It can't be helped."

In returning to Kumamoto City before dark we missed the picturesque sight of a summer evening when lights dot the fields of Amakusa. The lights are a way of fighting insects. An electric bulb over a large dish of oil attracts bugs, which end up in the oil.

Powerful insecticides imported from Germany are another way of coping. Rice plants get a thorough spraying after water is drained from the fields. Careless use of powerful bug killers caused deaths; now red flags are placed in fields to warn of danger.

Upon seeing the red flags a visitor to Japan remarked that Communism must have a great hold on Japanese farmers.

Maybe we should have given a couple of days to this island. How to pace ourselves on a long, complex journey is a problem. Even though reservations and appointments need to be made in advance, Father Flinn keeps saying, "Let it stay fluid." He feels more at ease with a loosely scheduled itinerary than I do.

As the bus rolled north from the island, off to the right was Yatsushiro where Father Joseph Greene is pastor. Yatsushiro reminded Father Flinn of a diary that tells of adversities Christians experienced even after official persecutions ceased.

While cleaning out the attic in his presbytery Father Eamonn Horgan, the Columban who was pastor there a few years ago, found a worm-eaten copybook in which the French priest Father Corre recorded his days after arriving in April of 1889 to establish a parish at Yatushiro.

The little Frenchman was a plucky fellow. Stones, angry shouts, and name-calling greeted him the first time he stood in the marketplace. He set off immediately to see the mayor, a kindly man, who sent him to the chief of police, who promised to protect both priest and property.

With such encouragement, Father Corre started visiting. He dropped in at all the schools in the area and spent much time with students and teachers. He must have had considerable charm because the diary reveals a gradual change of attitude toward him. The word "invitation" appears frequently, and important people of the town competed for his company.

Even so the French missionary's efforts were thwarted time and again when he tried to buy a plot of land on which to build a church. The tone is one of joy when he tells his diary that he has a site for a church and on it is an old storehouse that can be converted into a presbytery. A carpenter and his young son built, in six months, a mud-plastered church designed to hold eighty parishioners.

One of the people still fighting against Father Corre was a prominent figure in the Imperial army, Colonel Yoshinaga. When the colonel came to the presbytery with a prepared speech, the missionary listened with courtesy; when the Colonel had finished he spoke in detail of the Faith he had brought to Japan. Yoshinaga seemed mystified and asked if he might come again. After many return visits he was baptized, resigned his commission in the army, and worked as the parish catechist.

When Father Corre was transferred, a Japanese priest, Father Honda, became pastor. He continued the diary, not in French but in Latin.

New difficulties become evident in the diary in 1928. The militarists, in making preparations for war with the West, were suspicious of any Western influence. Police began to visit the presbytery to make searches and troubled the sisters with questions about what they taught in school.

How things went during the war is unclear; in those days it was unwise to put too much on paper. An old French priest who lived there at the time kept to himself and died before the war's end.

Father John O'Meara came to Yatsushiro, in 1951, the first Columban there. He found the same storehouse that Father Corre had moved into seventy years earlier and the same church. How decrepit! He donned dungarees, opened a toolkit, and made repairs.

Back in Kumamoto City in time for dinner. At mealtime the conversation of Columbans is lively; they have all had unusual experiences. Tonight someone observed that of late he sees fewer *rumpen*—conmen, tramps, hoboes.

Someone recalled a *rumpen* who had the kind of smile that got him past the housekeeper and into the reception room to see the pastor. The *rumpen* said he had come all the way from Nagasaki, but life had not treated him well in Kumamoto and now he wanted to return the hundred miles to home. How about train fare to Nagasaki?

The Columban decided that the conman would meet another soft touch along the way and so he contributed half of the fare. Two days later a letter of thanks came postmarked in a town exactly half way to Nagasaki.

April 27
Wednesday

Early this morning Father Flinn took me to a hospital, not far from the Columban church in Kumamoto City, to visit Father Michael Iwanaga, who for years was secretary to Archbishop Yamaguchi of Nagasaki.

Whenever I meet someone from Nagasaki I want to ask, "How did you escape the bomb, and how many relatives did you lose that morning?" On the walk to the hospital, Father Flinn said that Father Iwanaga was born sixty-eight years ago not far from the spot where the black pillar marks the epicenter of the explosion. His mother, his brother, and his brother's family died in the blast, and his friend, Archbishop Yamaguchi, lost ninety-four relatives.

Michael Iwanaga was saved because the Japanese army had drafted him. At war's end, he was in Indonesia and remained there a prisoner of the Australian army for eight months.

For two years Father has been bedridden. His right hand is paralyzed and his speech blurred. While lying there he must have thought often about the future of the Catholic Church in Japan, which he served long and well. I asked him about it.

"The Japanese are not against Christianity," he said. "They appreciate the good points in Christians, and Christians should appreciate the good points in them. I have no worry about the future.

"The conversions will not be sudden. Japan will move closer and closer to Christianity. The Church, like water under the earth, will provide refreshment. Priests and nuns will be like those at the well who bring water to the surface.

"At present there is a lack of faith because of materialism. That is how it is all over the world.

"There are plenty of religious vocations around Nagasaki. Why? People who have suffered for the Faith have a depth that does not diminish. All of Japan will be better spiritually after it suffers.

"If you have hope and faith then grace will do the work. God is aware of Japan—you must keep believing that. I am optimistic because I believe that God made people to save them, not to condemn them."

While walking to the hospital I had felt down and in no mood to visit the sick. But a half hour in the presence of a saintly man lifted my spirit.

Here in Kumamoto the people speak a dialect quite distinct from standard Japanese. Father Michael Molloy felt so frustrated, especially when trying to speak with the children, that he decided to go to school again. After summoning up enough courage he marched off to enroll at a local primary school.

At the principal's office he met Mr. Sugimura, tall and about fifty. The principal found it difficult to believe that the priest was from Ireland and that he really wanted to enroll at the school.

"We took the easy question first," said Father Molloy. "We soon agreed that Ireland was not Iceland and that it was not a part of England. However, it took some more meetings, some more cups of tea, and I suspect some sleepless nights for Mr. Sugimura before he became convinced that I really wanted to go back to school."

Once convinced he suddenly realized that here was a problem beyond the powers of any one man to cope with. He would need to call a meeting of all the teachers, then inform the Parent-Teacher Association, and then the City Board of Education. This took about a week. To the seeming delight of everyone at the end of that time the Columban was assigned to group three of class six.

Father Molloy tried to look brave as he walked beside the principal to the classroom. First there were introductions. The priest stood in front of the class looking into a roomful of excited, wide-open eyes. There were forty-five twelve-year-olds in the class. The principal said that the missionary would be a pupil in their language class, and that he was a gentleman, for all Englishmen are gentlemen, and then gave a five-minute lecture on the history of Ireland.

Father Molloy recalled the rest of the introduction with some uneasiness: "He told the overawed children how I had graduated from university and was humble enough to go to elementary school again. I had studied correct Japanese in Tokyo so on no account must anyone use the local dialect when speaking to me. From now on anyone getting lower marks in their tests than this foreigner would automatically fail. He said that in all of our previous meetings I had arrived exactly two minutes before the appointed time; so from now on he expected they would give me a good example by arriving on time."

An exceptionally large desk and chair loomed at the back of the room. Mr. Sugimura appointed two pupils to see that it was dusted daily. The Columban bowed all around and hurried to the back of the class to be out of sight as fast as possible.

The first few days were uneasy. Everyone took a peep back at the priest whenever the teacher was not looking. All ears practically vibrated with attention when Father Molloy had to read aloud or answer a question. Photographers disrupted classes by taking pictures of the unusual pupil.

"My teacher was Mrs. Nakao," said Father Molloy. "She had a sister-in-law living in Hawaii and got presents from her. One day she showed me something that had just arrived. Could I tell her what it was? It was a package of cake mix. I tried to explain the recipe in Japanese. I was never much of a hand at cooking and here I was trying to teach her how to make a cake. When the next parcel came I got a present of a box of cake mix."

The course began paying dividends outside of the classroom. Many people wrote to Father Molloy; some were interested in education, some in English, and some in Christianity. Locally he was getting more bows and greetings. There was a common bond between those who had a brother or sister, son or daughter, at the school with the foreigner. Suddenly the outsider was beginning to feel at home.

Father Molloy remembers his classmates with affection. "No group of children I have known were more polite and naturally courteous. I often thought of what the poet said: the grace of God is in courtesy."

The Columbans opened Boys Town in Kumamoto in 1955. They taught boys, ages seven to eighteen, farming and carpentry along with the more traditional courses in reading, writing, and arithmetic.

In November 1977 Takayoshi Watanabe became a priest, the first to be ordained of the more than three hundred boys who have passed through Boys Town. It is fitting that Father Takayoshi would then be appointed chaplain of the institution. (It has also become a home for girls since the Columbans turned it over to an order of Japanese Sisters.)

Before Takayoshi was born, his father died. His mother already had two small children; when the boy was eighteen months old she found it necessary to put him into an orphanage run by Franciscan Missionary Sisters of Mary. When Takayoshi reached seven the sisters sent him to the Columbans at Boys Town.

The child greatly admired Father George Bellas, a Columban from New York, a strict but kind father. He looked forward to the visits of Father Maurice Maloney, from Australia, whose conjuring tricks fascinated him, and of Father Patrick Diamond, from Ireland, who taught him to play soccer.

The kindness of the missionaries impressed the boy. In his talk at his First Mass Father Takayoshi said, "I will always remember something that might have influenced me to be a priest; it was the way Father Bellas would come each day to visit me or any of the other boys whenever we were sick in bed with a cold or something. He would try to cheer us up, but better still before leaving he would give his blessing to each one of us. That impressed me because I thought, 'That is something that only a priest can do.'"

A Columban observed: "It seems like a kind gesture of Providence, and particularly appropriate, that Father Takayoshi should be appointed chaplain at Boys Town at this time. Just when Father Bellas, who lived and worked there for twenty-two years was due to leave, a boy from among his first youngsters was ordained and took his place as chaplain. The wheel had come full circle."

In late morning Father Flinn and I took a bus from Kumamoto City northward to Fukuoka City. Off to the right was Mount Aso, a volcano with the largest crater in the world.

One day Fathers George Bellas, Bede Cleary, and an American Army chaplain decided to climb to the summit. They drove along a winding tree-lined road out to where there are vast expanses of land almost uninhabited, a rarity in overcrowded Japan. A small herd of cattle huddled by a shallow lake. The quiet of the grave and an intense loneliness hung like a miasma over the hilly place.

Mount Aso scatters dust for miles, making the land poor for cultivation and almost useless for human habitation. The only signs of activity, at the point where the crater begins, are vendors at a souvenir store and cooks in a restaurant.

The three priests picked their way up a path along the mountainside scorched black and covered with tortuous masses of lava and stone. At the edge of the crater, which is about fifteen miles across, they looked with uneasiness down at a solid spout of flame and smoke rising with incredible force from the bowels of the earth. The roar was terrifying. Every now and then there was a slight lull, followed by an eruption of red hot rocks sailing up through the smoke.

Japanese selling souvenirs at the site told the priests that they could get an official stamp proving that they had really been there. The vendors said that they live all day with the volcano, except when it becomes unusually vicious, then they retreat until some tranquility returns.

In Fukuoka City we walked through Minoshima, the poorer section, guided by a church steeple, searching for Father Joseph Finnerty, one of the Columban pioneers in Japan.

At the school yard we found an exuberance of kindergarten kids. Japanese children under six seem more doll-like than any other children in the world. These had come to school wearing navy blue uniforms with white blouses or shirts. At the classroom door were kept two pairs of slippers, one pair for inside and one for outside. The children changed their blue berets for orange, red, peach, or green caps, indicating the class to which each belonged. There they were, ages three to five, a colorful effervescence.

When Father Flinn asked where we might find Father Finnerty, a tiny boy, destined for leadership, took off for the classroom to pass the word to teacher.

We stood there admiring a charming little church, something out of a fairy tale. It was moved to this spot thirty years ago; twenty years earlier it had been built near Bishop Breton's residence for the Sisters of the Visitation, an all-Japanese society founded in California in 1915.

When Father Finnerty appeared, he took us for a walk through his parish near the heart of the city. His 150 parishioners, mostly old people who date back to the time the church was moved, operate tiny shops, with open fronts, on narrow back streets. Many have come from Nagasaki to work at jobs nobody else wants. Some are butchers, a trade looked down upon in the Orient. In speaking of parishioners both priests used the word *Burakumin*, later I was to find out what that word meant.

"These people are so busy making a living that they have no time to be active in the church," Father Finnerty said. "They support the church to the best of their ability, but it is the fees from the kindergarten that keep us out of the red. There are about 120 children each paying $60 a month.

"Scarcely a child in the kindergarten is Christian. Most of their parents are Shinto or Buddhist.

"The biggest difficulty now is lack of time. When we came to Japan in

1948 people had no money, but they had plenty of time. Now they have money, but no time. People were more spiritually inclined just after the war."

In those days Father Finnerty was learning the language in a hit-or-miss manner. He would write out his sermons in English and have them translated into Japanese.

When he was pastor of a place known as Sin City East, his parish led all others in converts. That indicates, he said, that sin and virtue live close together.

The tempo of conversions was at its highest during the American Occupation from 1945 until 1952. "That was an artificial period in Japanese culture," said the missionary. "But after the treaty was signed the Japanese felt that Japan was again Japan. Between 1952 and 1964, the year of the Tokyo Olympics, the Japanese were rediscovering themselves.

"Nationalism is on the rise now. There is a great upsurge of propaganda—Japanese food is best, Japanese products are best, Japanese life is best.

"Although we are at low ebb now as far as conversions are concerned, the people are easier to associate with when you meet them. Their inferiority complex is gone. There is plenty of indifference, but no anti-Christian feeling. The only time some conflict might arise would be over a mixed marriage. In such a showdown the new Buddhist sect, the Soka Gakki, would be apt to win. The Soka Gakki have slipped in recent years; politically they were much stronger a decade or more ago."

Father Finnerty, like many people over here, greatly admires the way General MacArthur handled the Japanese at the end of the war.

"It was a stroke of genius that he saw the wisdom of preserving the Emperor. He made the Emperor come to visit him, but after that he did nothing to demean him."

This brought to mind that Pearl Buck had described the American occupation as "humane, considerate, and constructive beyond any known in history." She said it worked because of the Japanese tradition of courtesy and the American habit of good will and generosity.

The *Burakumin* in the back streets of Fukuoka City stuck in my mind. Father Flinn said he has written a magazine article about them, as I might have guessed; he has written about almost every phase of life in Japan.

"In physical features and in language they are the same as any other Japanese," he said. "Yet they are looked down upon. How this started we don't know. Perhaps they were butchers and tanners who fell into disrepute when in the sixth century Buddhists started the admonition, 'Thou shalt not kill anything.' "

Years ago there was a strict division of labor and status. Below the imperial family and nobility were four classes—warrior, peasant, artisan, merchant. Under them were two sub-groups—*Hinin*, composed of beggars, prostitutes, and traveling entertainers, and *Eta*, those who dealt with dead animals. Such nonpeople were forced to live in designated areas and were forbidden to marry other Japanese. Even today eighty percent of three million *Burakumin* live in western Japan, mainly in six thousand hamlets.

"The ancient myths persist," said Father Flinn. "References are made to their 'unjapaneseness' and to their 'biological inferiority,' but the only real differences are social, economic, and educational. Poverty has kept many from completing their nine years of compulsory education. Dropouts find it hard to get good jobs. The initial handicap perpetuates itself.

"Even though the 1871 reform gave equality before the law, and no one is forced into a designated area, you still find *Burakumin* living in ghettoes. They are butchers, leather workers, shoe shiners, porters, odd jobbers, or ragpickers. You won't find many in modern factories. That's because big companies depend on harmony in the plant, and the presence of a *Burakumin* is offensive to some workers and customers."

There have been generals, university professors, and politicians of *Burakumin* origin. When they escape from their hamlets, they try to obliterate their tracks and have their children educated with special care, living in the fear that their secret will be discovered three generations later.

The opposition is great when a *Burakumin* wants to marry someone from outside the group. Relatives and friends try forced separation and ostracism. This gets so severe that sometimes the two young people commit suicide.

"About half the marriages of non-Christians that I performed in Imafuku were in the church because the young couple could not get consent for a traditional Japanese wedding," said Father Flinn. "I remember one lad who lost his job the day after he married a girl suspected of being a *Burakumin*. The boss was a friend of the lad's father who resented the marriage.

"Many *Burakumin* folk enter the church. They are accepted on equal terms. No discrimination is made against them, until marriage is mentioned. Then you realize that the ills of society are real among Christians, too.

"Many *Burakumin* people have a deep inferiority complex, even a persecution complex. Even when they enter religious life it shows up. They are suspicious, sensitive, and unpredictable. Scars of long victimization are there."

Japan is not trying to sweep this problem under the mat. Nor is it any longer the "unmentionable" problem that it used to be. Each year parents, teachers, and other interested persons meet to see what can be done. The idea that legislation and government grants will bring assimilation has been discarded. That just doesn't work.

Emphasis is placed on getting the *Burakumin* to take pride in their origins. The aim is to have the history of the *Burakumin* people taught in schools and in adult education programs. This does not mean developing a melting pot but giving a deep sense of identity among *Burakumin* youth.

The people who are working on this problem feel that the *Burakumin* must learn to accept the fact that they were born into a certain community. Then they can maintain their identity, their integrity, and their pride. This is based on the psychological principle that to be accepted by others one must first sincerely accept oneself.

I asked Father Finnerty how he feels about the future of Christianity in Japan.

"I am optimistic about it," he said. "Of course it will have to do a lot of reflecting about itself. It is still too westernized."

He is aware that when a religion is introduced it changes the prevailing culture only somewhat. The culture of a country is so durable that if any religious movement is to succeed it must adapt itself to the prevailing way and even cherish it.

April 28
Thursday

There is a Japanese saying, "If you have eyes to see, go to Kyoto." We went to Kyoto from Fukuoka City in three hours and thirty-seven minutes. One of the bullet trains hurtled us, at speeds up to 130 miles an hour, through innumerable tunnels and under the sea to get from the island of Kyushu to that of Honshu.

Father Flinn recalled a trip of similar length that took thirty-six hours just after the war. He stood all the way in a coach so tightly packed that to reach the restroom was nearly impossible.

What a difference now that these bullet trains, running twelve minutes apart, zip across Japan without even human intervention. Oh, there is an operator looking out the front window, but a computer does the work.

On one run the operator got himself locked inside the restroom, but the computer went ahead and made all the starts and stops and eased into Tokyo right on the second. The passengers were unaware of this until they read about it in the newspaper next day, then they became incensed, complaining in letters to the editor how their lives had been endangered.

At Hiroshima the bullet made a brief pause. Seen from the high trestle the city looks like so many concrete filing cabinets, banal and ugly. Father Flinn told me that Hiroshima has vulgarized its tragedy. Two million tourists visit there each year to see the Mount of the Dead, the Hiroshima Maidens, and to go to cafes and nightclubs with such names as The Fireball Bar.

In Kyoto's railroad station we were both startled by the construction that has taken place in recent years. What used to be a simple station stretches on and on underground, making you aware that you are entering a city of a million and a half people.

What to see? That is always a problem in Kyoto, the city of abundance: 253 Shinto shrines, 1,600 Buddhist temples and palaces and pavilions galore built by emperors and shoguns.

What I like most is walking the narrow streets in the old neighborhoods, enjoying the tiny gardens, and the houses with such right proportions, and the wonderful roof patterns seen from commanding ground.

We told a taxi driver to take us to some part of town that still reflects the old Kyoto. He drove us to Kiyomizu Temple in the Higashi mountains where there is a grand view of the whole of Kyoto City with mountains in the distance.

This temple was founded in the year 798 and after being destroyed by fire was rebuilt in 1633. It consists of a *Romon*, a two-storied gate; a *Sanjunoto*, a three-storied pagoda; and a *Shoro*, a belfry.

Trying to describe Kiyomizu Temple is frustrating because the whole is far greater than the parts. If you tell of the stepping stones, the waterfall, and the roof thatched with layers of cypress bark, you know that they simply do not convey the feelings you get when you are there.

Perhaps the best way to share the experience is by indirection; to say, for instance that the Japanese like things *odayaka*. Be it seasoning in food, the weather, or the personality of a friend, let it be *odayaka*—mild, calm, tranquil, not excessive, not blatant, not abrasive.

Although this temple complex covers quite a bit of hillside, it has a feeling of restraint. The Japanese like things lean. In poetry, *haiku* passes along a mood in three lines of seventeen syllables; in *ikebana* or flower arranging, no bud or leaf is allowed in the arrangement except those which are essential to its full grace; in *Noh* plays the actors avoid superfluous gestures; in ink painting, *sumi-e*, all clutter is shunned. Straight to the heart is the way of Japanese art.

Art is not for the sake of art in Japan, but art is for the sake of life. Everyday things have style. The ticket, for example, that admits you to a temple, or a museum, or a garden is so beautifully designed that you hesitate to throw it away, and end up using it as a bookmark, one that brings pleasure at each glance.

Kiyomizu-Dera has tranquility, and a sense of rightness, and here every prospect pleases.

The romance of temple bells and the heady aroma of incense are enchanting. Few sounds are more solemn than the mellow booming of a temple bell.

Father Flinn said the enormous bronzes should be called gongs because they are struck from without by a horizontally suspended beam.

Years ago he knew a Buddhist priest who kept appealing for funds for a bell even though his temple needed repair. The Buddhist repeated, "It takes a temple bell to keep true religion in the hearts of people, and to pass along Buddha's message to all."

Just before midnight on December 31, all of Japan's 88,000 temple bells start ringing out the old year with 108 peals. Buddhists say that each peal of the *Joya no kane*, or New Year's Eve bell, banishes one of the 108 vices which beset the human race. It is during the chiming that Japanese make their resolutions.

The Japanese love of flowers is especially evident here in Kyoto: the policeman on duty with a potted flower at his feet; women hurrying to and from classes in flower arrangement; children wandering through fields studying plants and insects; lovely gardens around the poorest homes.

"Two things it is no crime to take," they tell you with a smile, "a flower and a photograph." And another of their sayings: "To the man who comes to take our flowers we give a cup of tea." In other words anyone who would wish to have a flower can't be all bad.

It is encouraging how much the Japanese can build and still leave the countryside undisturbed. They do not cut down a tree unless it is unavoidable, and often they forego building on a suitable site in order to save a tree.

Trees and flowers are usual topics of conversation. The smallest children can name the flowers and insects found in the neighborhood. Insects are playthings to be collected tenderly, not as pests to be destroyed on sight. Children gather armored beetles, snakes, bullfrogs, and spiders, some of them fighting spiders to be put into a ring.

A Columban said, "On one occasion I was entertaining visitors in my presbytery when my attention was distracted by some magazines which seemed to be wandering around the table. I found two shrimps underneath, left there by boys from next door. The visitors, two ladies, had known all along, but did not think the matter worth mentioning. St. Francis of Assisi would feel at home among such people."

Japanese poetry concerns itself with flowers, wildlife, and the changes of the seasons. The Japanese love of nature is evident in two lines of a poem:

> *The morning glory twining binds my well-rope*
> *And I must borrow water.*

The thought is of a housewife going early one morning to draw water from her well and finding that the morning glory had wound itself around the rope the night before. Rather than break it she goes next door for water.

The Japanese love the world that God has made.

Every now and then when walking down the street, Father Flinn turns to find me missing Usually I have stopped to admire a *bonsai* tree.

The secret of *bonsai* growing, I am told, is based on a close observation of trees in their natural state. The perfect *bonsai* should bear all the characteristics of the tree it miniatures; it should change with the seasons, flower, bear fruit, and shed leaves if deciduous.

The normal height of such a dwarf is about two feet, a convenient size for handling. The trays and pots in which they are grown are shallow and contain no more soil than is absolutely needed.

The trees are kept small by judicious trimming and pruning of roots and branches. They need just enough sunlight and wind, and as little moisture as possible, to stop superfluous growth. The leaves can be reduced only so much for that reason it is necessary to choose small-leaved trees with dense twigs, such as pine, fir, and larch.

The grower shapes the tree through pruning, bending, and twisting. A spiral wire wound around the branches or stem forces them into the proper shape, and once the form becomes permanent the wire is removed.

Such little trees can live for centuries. Four hundred years ago one of the *shoguns* gave a *bonsai* to the emperor. It is alive today in the Imperial palace in Tokyo.

Every afternoon here in Kyoto, about the time that school is out, the clop-clop-clop of the *kami shibaisan* or paper showman's stick, is heard in the narrow, winding streets. Children, hearing the sound, run to their mothers to beg a few *yen* and dash toward the paper showman's bicycle.

"*Sah, sah*, what will you have today!" he calls. "A stick of candy? A piece of cuttlefish?"

The children crowd around thrusting their money towards him as he opens the wooden box on the back of the bicycle. They peer eagerly into the drawers. In the top one are the ten-by-twelve-inch colored pictures he uses to tell his tales. In the next two are tins of hard candy, soft rice candy, and paper-thin squares of dried cuttlefish.

The children are anxious to hear what happened to the little girl in the story he began yesterday, or how the brave *samurai* warrior fared when trapped in the enemy's castle. The *kami shibai* man knows what pleases his audience and so there are sword fights galore in the tales he tells.

When all the children have been supplied with something to eat, the *kami shibai* man slides in a set of pictures at the back of the box and the show is on. Now the showman really comes to life. He usually has four stories to tell and he takes the parts of all the characters who appear in them. He becomes the brave *samurai* charging with his sword or the gentle maiden weaving cloth at home. He is suddenly a laughing woman or a cross old man. Sometimes he is more fun to watch than the pictures.

The showman knows how to keep his audience coming back. He leaves his heroes in perilous predicaments.

He calls out, "What will happen to Kichisaburo? To be continued tomorrow." Then he hurries away to entertain the children on another street. Tomorrow he will be back at the same minute on the same spot. Before long the *kami-shibai* men will have vanished; their number dwindles each year.

Tonight we went to a castle to see several demonstrations, each reflecting some aspect of Japan's culture. They ranged from the gentleness of the tea ceremony and flower arranging to the more hectic activity of Kabuki theater and martial arts.

Afterward I was amazed once more at the amount of information Father Flinn has accumulated about Japanese culture. He has written so many magazine ariticles on the subject that he is able to give me the kind of detailed information that I could not get from demonstrations in the castle.

"Tea served in a Japanese tea ceremony is so thick and strong that it is not recommended for anyone suffering from insomnia," said Father Flinn. "Traditionally it was brewed this way in China to keep Buddhist monks awake during their long hours of meditation."

The first tea used in Japan was imported by Buddhist monks who had it sent from China by their confreres. Following the Chinese custom, monks of the Zen sect in Japan gathered in the temple to drink tea from a single bowl in a solemn ceremony before meditation.

The ritual developed into a social pastime during the fifteenth century and by the sixteenth the *chanoyu*, or tea ceremony, had become so involved that the courts of high officials had masters of ceremonies to preside over the complicated ritual.

The tea is served according to sets of rules which vary with the occasion, the standing of the guests, or even the season of the year. The ceremony, if carried out strictly, requires a special set of rooms. The tea room proper, about nine feet square, is designed to accommodate not more than five persons. An anteroom provides a place to wash and arrange the tea utensils before they are brought in. There should be a portico where guests wait until they receive the invitation to enter. A garden path connects the portico with the tea room.

The tea, a powdered green variety called *uji*, is served to guests in a common bowl.

Father Leo Baker remembers the first tea ceremony he attended more than thirty years ago. "A row of cushions had been placed in a straight line on the floor and a tiny charcoal fire was burning brightly in an earthenware container set up near the cushions. The teacher arrived and took up her position by the fire while we arranged ourselves on the cushions.

"The teacher began to arrange the bowls and other utensils with slow precise movements. Every gesture was performed gracefully and deliberately according to a definite set of rules. The idea behind all of this is to produce a spirit of composure and quiet peacefulness in the performer of the ceremony and, to a degree, in all taking part."

When the tea was ready, the teacher poured some of it into a bowl and handed it to the hostess, who took it with approved gestures and exclamations of appreciation. Then she drank it slowly and finished the last mouthful with a loud sucking noise that was meant to show how much she enjoyed it. Everyone else followed suit.

"I was charmed by the rhythm and gracefulness of it all," said Father Baker. "I think that it really must have a composing effect upon those who carry it out in all of its exacting detail. The whole ceremony performed properly takes about four hours."

In demonstrating martial arts, a master of *Iai-do* threw a piece of paper into the air, drew a long samurai's sword from its sheath, cut the paper in half and replaced the sword before the paper touched the floor.

A master of *karate* brought down the edge of his hand upon a stack of eight roof tiles and shattered them. I flinched with empathy. Another shattered eight tiles with his head. Ouch!

Father Flinn knows the scientific explanation behind this: "The human body can deliver about two hundred joules, units of energy. It takes less than ten joules of energy to crack a concrete block.

"When a block is struck it is like a thick rubber band oscillating at two hundred cycles a second. A *karate* blow stretches them one millimeter to their breaking point. If the blow is not hard enough the block snaps back against the hand to cause pain."

So the practitioner concentrates. His timing and striking power must be just right. He centers his breath in his abdomen. His entire frame quivers in anticipation, a spring ready for action. The mind signals; the hand strikes. Wood, stone, or roof tiles shatter under a well-delivered blow. Battle cries from deep in the abdomen help the striker get the job done.

Father Flinn said that the movies of Bruce Lee made the martial arts a craze all over the world. I used to see Lee in movie ads, but know little about him.

"He was a *kung-fu* wizard," said Kevin Flinn. "Yet he was less than five feet eight inches tall and weighed only 150 pounds. His hands were like hammers. Like a drilling machine. Palm hits. Wrist hits. Reverse and horizontal punches. He flew through the air; his kicks were delivered high and low with astounding rapidity. With a one-inch punch he could floor a large opponent.

"Overnight he became a household word."

I was surprised to learn that *kung-fu* and Zen meditation originated from the same Shaolin Temple in China. What connects violence and tranquility; the martial arts and meditation?

Father Flinn said that it started in 520 A.D. when a little monk from India, a Zen master, went into a cave near a monastery of Sacred Song Mountain, in Henan Province, China. After nine years he emerged as a hard taskmaster.

"The Indian monk saw that most Chinese monks had no idea of the truth of Buddhism. They merely indulged in ritual and intellectual pursuits. He devised a new technique to help the monks gain enlightenment—that intuitive leap to wisdom. He adopted the *yin* and *yang* theory of Chinese Taoism. The theory is that primal unity is composed of two forces—*yin*, receptive, calm, cold, dark, and female; and *yang*, bright, warm, productive, and male. These primary forces—one passive and one active—are not in conflict with each other, but are constantly at interplay in the cosmos, complementing each other. They need each other. Everything in human beings and in the universe is influenced by harmony and tension between *yin* and *yang*."

To use both primary forces, the Indian monk decided that the *yin* element should perfect the spirit and the *yang* element the body. So for the spirit he developed *kung-an* (or *koan*) exercises which grappled with unanswerable questions; for the body, *kung-fu* with its more than one hundred movements.

"As an example of how Zen influences the martial arts look at it this way," said Father Flinn. "Zen Buddhist philosophy abhors attachments. In the martial arts the mind is emptied, free of attachments. By placing it nowhere it can be everywhere. Placed nowhere, the mind is diffused throughout the body. Stretched out. Totally unfettered. It is then free to serve arms, legs, eyes. If one concentrates, for instance, on the movement of the sword, or on the enemy's sword, the mind is somewhat fettered. To be ready for any attack from any direction, there must be an inner freedom."

The *kanku* symbolic pose expresses the ideals of *karate*. The hands are together above the head, palms outward. The practitioner looks at the sky through the triangle formed by thumbs and fingers. The pose expresses self-identification with nature, tranquility, and the wish for harmony.

Father Flinn hopes that the spiritual side of all this will resurface. He said that the current abbot at the monastery in China, where the Indian monk developed *kung-an* and *kung-fu*, predicted: "*Kung-fu* boxing and Zen meditation do seem contradictory. Violence versus tranquility. But each was meant to bring a different sort of peace. They were born together and developed together over the centuries. I think they will become popular again together."

After watching a demonstration of *Kabuki* in the castle tonight Father Flinn said: "Most people know a fair amount about *Kabuki*. Foreigners are facinated by its spectacular plays, costuming, stage effects, and dance sequences. *Kabuki* is of the people. It is down to earth, always making concessions to what people like. It is direct in its blood-and-thunder presentations. *Kabuki* is entertainment but *Noh* is an experience. *Noh* is ritual filled with symbols. For instance, touching the fingers to the eyes conveys weeping. A fan in an actor's hand may serve as a sword or a wine cup. A step or two to one side might convey a journey to China. A folded robe might be accepted as a woman who is ill."

From the way he talked I think he likes *Kabuki* better than *Noh*.

Kyoto had been the capital of Japan for more than a thousand years when, in 1868, the Meiji government moved to Edo and changed the name of that place to Tokyo, meaning Eastern capital. That was the best thing that could happen to Kyoto. The move cleared out most of the politicians, captains of industry, wheeler-dealers and militarists.

If I were going to live in Japan I would perfer Kyoto or Nagasaki. They have something for the soul. Tokyo has everything for the body.

70

The "Daibutsu" of Kamakuru, a bronze statue of Amida Buddha cast in 1252, which at 42 feet 6 inches is the second largest in Japan.

"Virgin in Disguise"—a statue of the Madonna with child, assuming the appearance of Kannon, the Buddist Goddess of Mercy.

"Here lie Ogasawara Genya and his wife, Miyako, their six sons, three daughters, and four servants, martyred, Kumamoto Castle, December 23, 1635."

Burial site in Ryujin of downed American flyers.

Brother Zeno selecting boots for distribution to the poor.

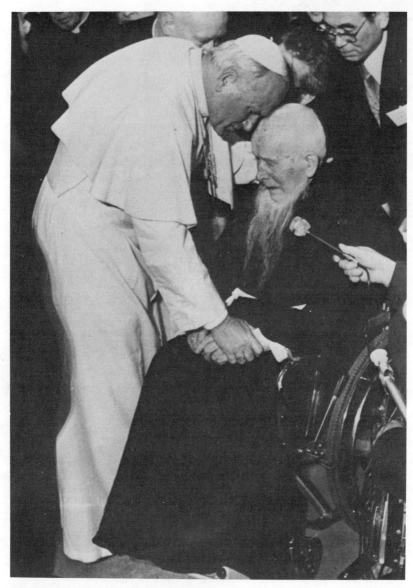

Pope John Paul II greeting his compatriot,
Br. Zeno, in Toyko Cathedral, February 1981.

Fujiama

Crowds climbing Mt. Fuji

Tukayoshi Watanabe upon entering Boys Town at the age of seven.

Father Watanabe,
the first Boys Town
alumnus to be ordained.

Gardening at Boys Town

The Boys Town
chapel in Kumamoto

A wedding performed by Fr. Kevin Flynn

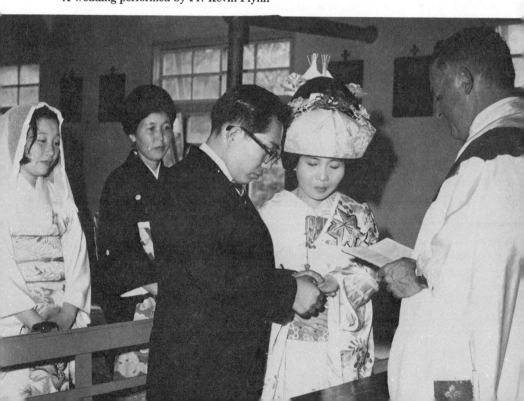

A family places the ashes of a deceased relative
in the church crypt.

A kindergarten group in Nokasanji

Buying goldfish in Tokyo

Zori shoes at steps of a school

The Karate Club of Sophia University, Tokyo

Japan's "bullet" train

The art of *ikebana* or flower arranging

The Toyko Fish Market

Rice fields in and around a village

April 29
Friday

A guidebook published by Japan Air Lines warns that when holidays follow close upon each other, "be prepared for all public transportation to be packed to the ceilings and windows—literally." A period "to be avoided at all costs," continues the guidebook, is Golden Week which begins with the Emperor's Birthday on April 29 and continues through Children's Day on May 5. "This is the time for many Japanese to discover their own country, or for some to take trips overseas."

This morning's newspaper estimates that fifty-two million Japanese will travel during Golden Week beginning today. Many of them were on the Kinki Nippon train during the thirty-three minute ride last night from Kyoto to Nara.

Today the Emperor is eighty-two. He lives in the 284-acre enclosure of the Imperial palace, which on the map seems the center of Tokyo. The spiderweb of streets radiating from the enclosure is symbolic of the central place the Emperor holds, or used to hold, in Japanese life.

Japan has had only one line of rulers in the 2,000 years of her national existence. Emperor Hirohito, of the oldest family in the nation, is the 124th in the line of succession.

The Emperor, a lifelong student of marine biology, spends much of his time in his private laboratory. He knows more than anyone in the world about jellyfish and related creatures and has published sixteen books in the field. Within the enclosure is a small rice paddy which, I hear, the Emperor himself tends.

In the West we had forgotten about the Emperor until 1970 when Yukio Mishima, an eminent Japanese writer, committed ritual suicide. This was a gesture meant to dramatize his desire to bring back traditions of Old Japan and the absolute rule of the Emperor.

Most Japanese, I suppose, are content to accept the Emperor as "the symbol of the State and of the unity of the people." That is the role the postwar constitution assigned to him thirty-six years ago this May.

The *Japan Times* says that a bundle of yellow papers has been discovered in the National Archives in Washington, D.C. telling of the divided feelings of the Japanese after Hirohito had broadcast his country's surrender to bring the Second World War to an end. A cardboard box contains 318 letters and postcards addressed to General Douglas MacArthur, Supreme Commander of the Allied Powers, who in that capacity wielded absolute authority over occupied Japan.

The appeals for leniency far outnumbered those asking that the Emperor be punished. While private citizens were asking that Hirohito not be tried as a war criminal, the Soviet Union, Nationalist China, some members of the United States congress, and the Communist Party in Japan were calling for his prosecution.

A Tokyo woman in pleading with MacArthur not to put the Emperor on trial put her thumb mark dipped in blood next to her signature. While another letter, addressed "to the great disciple of human love, His Excellency MacArthur," urged punishment for the Emperor and his family "who deceived the natives of Japan for 3,000 years." Another proposed that MacArthur take the Emperor to Washington to apologize to President Truman in a worldwide broadcast.

On October 11, 1946, Joseph Kennan, the chief prosecutor at the International Military Tribunal for the Far East, announced that the Emperor would not be tried as a war criminal.

A Japanese lady told Father Michael O'Neill that the Japanese took defeat with grace because of the Emperor. "We obey him. It is the Emperor's will that we should be disciplined and orderly in defeat."

Father O'Neill found this an illuminating remark. He knew that Japan's situation at the end of the war held the seeds of chaos. Her cities and industries were destroyed; her army, largely intact and undefeated in the field, disbanded; and eight million Japanese were repatriated to an already overcrowded country. Here was a proud nation, at the height of her power as conqueror and colonizer, being occupied by a foreign power for the first time in history.

"The Japanese seemed endowed with hard realism," the Columban said. "Their attitude seemed to be, 'We lost the war, and that's that.' "

A missionary sister who had spent more than twenty years among the Japanese warned Father O'Neill not to be deceived by apparent stoicism. With great sympathy and admiration she said: "Now as never before they are showing what character and reserves of strength they possess. But they are suffering behind smiling faces. The foreigner thinks that a smiling face betokens a happy heart. Not so. It is part of the Japanese code to conceal one's real feelings."

An Englishman said to Father O'Neill: "I have seen them at the height of their power and I came to dislike them intensely. Returning to Japan I now see them in defeat, and, Father, they are a great people."

One wonderful thing about Nara, where we went next, is that it is so compact you can walk to wherever you want to go. This reduces traffic. Buses and taxis are not so dense as to clutter the beauty of parks and gardens.

Father Flinn and I walked to Isuien Garden at opening time, and had the place to ourselves. Father is planning to write a magazine piece about Japanese gardens; so he spent much of the morning photographing scenes in Isuien. He will never find one better for his purpose.

At their best Japanese gardens are graced with a mood of security, privacy, and antiquity. Scale and proportion have a "rightness" about them, a feeling that nothing can be rightly added and nothing rightly taken away.

Each turn of the head changes the angle of vision, yet every prospect has unity because something dominates—a pond, or a lantern, or a twisted tree. All are held in harmony with stones of just the right shape, groundcover of the right density, and houses of right proportions. Even people on the paths contribute to the aesthetic whole.

The seasons, too, are considered: green in time turns scarlet and snow simplifies shapes. Over it all hangs the spirit of nostalgia. Call it a joy tinged with sadness.

From the garden we walked through Nara Park, where nearly a thousand deer roam. Here the holiday crowd was most evident. School children in droves! Father Flinn said that on the day that children start going to school they begin paying into a trip fund. This gives them trips in the sixth grade of primary, then at the end of junior high, and at the end of the senior high.

We went from Nara Park to nearby Todai-ji temple. What a remarkable quietening effect the dark interior has on the children. This is the world's largest wood structure and it houses the world's largest bronze Buddha, fifty-three feet tall. The building and the Buddha were completed more than twelve hundred years ago.

In the northwest corner of the Todai-ji temple grounds is a wooden building, Shoso-in, that housed ten thousand objects of art for twelve centuries, preserving them remarkably well. This seems impossible considering how much humidity Japan suffers. Japanese architects long ago devised an ingenious plan to control the humidity. They assembled timbers in a triangular form so that as the humidity increased outdoors the wood expanded to force the narrow surfaces against each other and so stop the flow of air into the building; when the outside humidity was low the timbers shrank, allowing a space between them that dry air could enter. So the interior was at the proper humidity through the centuries.

These objects of art were a worry to scholars when Japan and the United States went to war in December 1941. What if bombers came? Packaging the treasures required great care and progress was slow.

While this was happening in Japan, a professor in a classroom at Harvard said to his students: "Sooner or later you may go to fight in Japan. But please bear in mind the location of Japanese artwork. Especially remember Kyoto and Nara."

The professor was Dr. Langdon Warner. He had become an expert on Japanese art during his many visits to the Orient over a period of forty years. Fortunately, Dr. Warner was appointed to the Asian department of a government committee in charge of protecting art in the countries at war.

He listed the sites of valuable treasures that deserved protecting and indicated degrees of merit by drawing one, two, or three stars next to the sites. Todai-ji temple and the wood building near it received three stars.

Nara and Kyoto escaped bombings after Dr. Warner explained to several generals in the Pentagon that these cultural treasures if destroyed would be a loss to all humanity, one that could never be redeemed.

In 1963 the Shoso-in treasures were moved to new fireproof, earthquake-proof concrete buildings next to the ancient wood structure. Will these repositories, blessed with modern science and sophisticated technology, preserve the treasures for another twelve hundred years?

A statue to Dr. Langdon Warner stands in Nara.

(Lately a high-school teacher, Ryo Suzuki, said that his research shows that Nara was bombed fourteen times. The U.S. occupation forces, he said, created the Warner myth to establish the image that Americans care about art.)

Since Nara was spared the bombings, it has more traditional homes than the large new cities where the trend is toward Westernization.

Upon entering a traditional home the first thing you do is to take off your shoes and leave them inside the door. You step up about a foot into a room where the floor is covered with straw mats, called *tatami*, three inches thick, six feet long, and three wide. Furnishings are sparse—a few tables a foot high and several cushions. No chairs.

The cultured Japanese collect scrolls, *kakemono*. Each month they select one to hang in the *tokonoma*, the alcove of honor, the most important corner of the old-fashioned home.

Since there are no chairs one is expected to sit in the Japanese manner, an art acquired with pain if you are an outsider. On a thin cushion placed on the matting you are to kneel and sit back on your heels.

"Their muscles have been trained to it from childhood, while mine have not," said a Columban. "In the early days I cut my visits short, limiting them to the length of time my legs could bear the aches. About ten minutes."

Upon leaving you find your shoes set out, facing the door, so that you can step right into them. The better homes have a shoe horn, two feet long hanging at the door, so you need not bend down.

Nara like Kyoto is a center for ceremonies and celebrations that keep alive Japan's traditions. We are aware of such dramatic ones as *O-Shogatsu*, New Year's, but there are many small, almost hidden celebrations not known abroad.

Hari-kuyo, for example, is a requiem for broken needles, celebrated February 8, especially in Buddhist schools for girls. Broken needles are stuck into a cake of *tofu*, white solidified bean curd, which is taken to a shrine.

Japanese women of the old school felt almost a mystic relationship with needles. Mary Ritchie, an American living in Japan, said that in the hands of a skillful seamstress needles fly so fast that they seem to have a life of their own. Needles, the same as people, differ one from another in strength and fineness. Before the days of mass manufacturing, making needles was so difficult that the craftsman felt he practically put some of his soul into each one.

Then there is the practical matter: a broken needle stuck in a cake of bean curd won't get lost in the *tatami* matting and end up stuck in some part of the anatomy.

Another celebration is *Hina-matsuri*, the Doll Festival, which coincides with Girl's Day on March 3. Dolls too expensive to play with are brought out and displayed on a series of stepped shelves for about two weeks.

Boy's Day, now usually called Children's Day, is celebrated with *koi-nobori*, colorful paper fish undulating in the warm air. Although the day is not until May 5 there are already many fish hanging from tall poles, but today they hang limp for lack of a breeze.

One fish flies for each male child in the family. The longest, as much as fifteen feet, is for the eldest; beneath it are proportionally smaller ones for the younger boys.

A song sung these days goes like this:

> *Flying high over the roof*
> *Is a family of carp streamers.*
> *Big, dark is daddy.*
> *Small, bright are children.*
> *All are making merry in the sky.*

Obon festival—the Buddhist feast of All Souls—may be the most picturesque festival of the year. Back in time out of mind the feast found its way from India by way of China to Japan. It was purely religious then, but now it is a social event as well.

Just as Christians return home for Christmas the Japanese make an effort to get home for Obon. They clean houses and gardens on August 13, the first day of the three-day festival. Family graves get plenty of care. Lighted lanterns are set at the doors of the houses to lead spirits safely home.

For the next two days ancestral spirits are much on everyone's mind. Rice, vegetables, fruit, and cake are placed on little family shrines, a focal point in every Buddhist home. A bucket of water stands at the door for the spirit's refreshment. At the end of Obon the votive foods are not eaten but are cast into the nearest river.

In Nagasaki where burial grounds are especially large there used to be the custom of holding parties at grave sites. The surroundings had no restraining effect on the gaiety of the gatherings; on the contrary, the merrier the party the more pleased the ancestral spirits were supposed to be.

The festival ends the night of August 15 with the picturesque ceremony called *Toro-nagashi*. Hundreds of little paper boats carry lighted lanterns down the rivers. When the last light burns out Obon is ended.

Tanabata, a festival held on the seventh day of the seventh month, is dying out in some places. The celebration grew from the legend that two stars, separated by the Milky Way, were able to meet once a year, on July 7, if rain did not fall that day. People used to gaze nervously at the summer sky and pray for fair weather so that the stellar lovers might meet.

Glenn Davis, an American teaching in Japan, said: "Members of the family wrote auspicious poems on strips of colored paper and decorated a bamboo cutting in the garden, much as Westerners decorate Christmas trees. Nowadays most Japanese are content to sit in air-conditioned living rooms and watch the spectacle on television rather than turn their gazes heavenward."

This evening we made the two-hour trip by train from Nara to Wakayama City. We will stay the night in the Columban parish in an old section of the city known as Yakata-machi.

Before the war the entire prefecture of Wakayama had only one priest and one church. Air raids reduced the mission to scorched ruins.

After the war, a priest came twice a month from Osaka. When a handful of Catholics gathered in a private home, the priest would open his valise, unfold vestments, and place the altar stone and altar cloth atop some piece of furniture.

Bishop Paul Taguchi of Osaka did not like this pray-and-run system, and so he asked the Columbans to open a church in Wakayama City. In 1948 Father Joseph O'Brien arrived as pastor, with his assistant Father Eric Brady.

Bishop Taguchi had a one-story house built for them on the site of the former church. A large room in the house served as a church for 130 Catholics.

In talking with the present pastor, Father Michael Healy, I asked how he feels about the place of the church in Japan.

"This mission has helped me sense the mystery of the redemption," he said. "Here the priesthood is a vocation, and not a matter of playing the role of priest. I mean by that, people do not hold you in high regard simply because you are a priest. While we have no statistics to show our achievements, I know in my heart that Christ is working out His redemption in Japan. Here I am more aware of the mystery of grace than I might be in some part of the world where a priest has more outward things happening in his favor. The mystery of God's Way is the thing that makes me pleased to be here in Japan."

April 30
Saturday

This morning—as sunny as all the others have been on this trip—our train passed the seaside town of Gobo on the way from Wakayama City to Tanabe. Gobo, a parish with some Columban history attached to it, is now being cared for by a Chinese volunteer, Father Peter Wang.

In 1954, disaster struck in the mountains, at a time when Fathers Kevin Lynch and James McGrath were stationed at Gobo. Up in Kawakami, two hundred villagers lost their lives when torrential rains brought floods and landslides. A man, who had lost father and sister, walked ten hours across the hills to bring the news to Gobo. After hearing his story, the two Columbans helped his stricken village so much that the people of Kawakami invited the priests to return and speak of religion.

In time the Columbans bought a small house in Kawakami and turned it into a church and rectory. Father McGrath became first pastor. Within two years his parishioners numbered sixty.

The men of Kawakami are woodcutters. When Columbans first went there the men rolled huge logs of cypress and cedar to the river's edge, strung them together into long serpentine rafts and rode down the river, balancing precariously while shooting rapids, on the two-day journey to Gobo. Now trucks bring the logs to the sea.

Woodcutters of Kawakami speak a dialect described as "backwoods Japanese." Father McGrath became one of the few priests in the world able to speak in the manner of Japanese backwoodsmen.

At Tanabe railroad station Father Michael Caufield, pastor of Saint Joseph's church, met us. We waited in his rectory until Father Eamonn Horgan came down by van to drive us to his mountain parish in Ryujin.

Once aboard the van, we wheeled along narrow mountain roads that have not a straight inch in them for twenty-seven miles. Father Flinn kept saying how much improved they are now over what they were when he was pastor of Ryujin.

"It's my kind of country!" said Father Horgan, a Columban from Kilkenny, as he gloried in the beauty of the scenery. "I can get used to a place like this in eighteen seconds. Some place else might take twenty-six seconds."

The Church of Saint Michael in Ryujin used to have more parishioners than the 307 it has today. Father Horgan explained: "As soon as jobs became available, if they paid well, the young left for Osaka and Nagoya. They found work in electrical manufacturing industries, in auto industries, and in construction work. There is no labor problem in Japan. There are about two percent unemployed, but anyone who really wants a job can find one.

"There is still a strong, pulsating Christian heart in this area. Sometimes a fellow comes up to me and says, 'I haven't been to church lately, but I'll be around one of these days.' "

Upon reaching Saint Michael's, which is surrounded by steep mountains dense in cypress and cedar, we met Father Horgan's menagerie—a Siamese cat with seven kittens, three rabbits, two bantam chickens, and a great shaggy Afghan hound.

Since Father Flinn was pastor of Ryujin for eighteen years he has many friends here, and so he took off to visit them just as darkness fell suddenly as it does in these mountains. When the night chill came down, Father Horgan and I settled close to the fire in his tiny living room. Well into the night he talked and I listened.

Looking into the fire he mused: "The Japanese have more of a feeling for religious things than do the Anglo-Saxons. Even a Japanese without any religious affiliation will show respect when stepping inside a church, but I have seen tourists from abroad acting without feeling in a shrine or temple.

"The Japanese concept of God may not be the same as ours, but they do have a concept of a Power that ought to be worshipped. I have never met a Japanese who gave me the faintest impression that he might be an atheist.

"They show more than a little interest in religion. Not to take it into their own lives but to study it as an aspect of the culture of other nations and of their own past."

Since the Second World War the govenment has been friendly toward all religious groups. As a country, Japan still maintains in magnificence its thousands of temples where old rituals are still honored.

And yet religion is missing in much of private and public life. If you ask a young Japanese what religion he professes he is apt to say: "My parents are Buddhist, but I am not a believer."

Father Horgan thinks that the breathtaking rate of change has had something to do with this. From being a staunchly isolationist nation, with a deep-rooted aversion to things foreign, Japan rapidly became expansionist. The leaders had to turn a nation of farmers, who accepted isolation, to a nation of mechanics and warriors full of aggression.

"To say that religion was the only means used to achieve this about-face would be oversimplifying the matter," said Father Horgan. "However, it is true that the leaders encouraged a loyalty to the Emperor which was akin to religious loyalty. For nearly half a century that was the nearest thing to religion that the great majority of Japanese had or were allowed to have."

The Emperor was regarded as something akin to a deity, with divine prerogatives and attributes. So he had a right to absolute loyalty and sacrifice from each of his subjects. It reached the point where the privilege of sacrificing one's life for the Emperor became something to prize.

Perhaps this was possible, said Father Horgan, because Shintoism had always stressed the divine ancestry of the Emperor and Japan had been delayed in its emergence from feudalism's demand of sacrifice and loyalty. And so until the end of the Second World War the rulers used as a powerful weapon the eagerness of the people to give all, life included, for the glory of country and Emperor.

Disillusionment came suddenly in August 1945. With the climax of the war, a grim "Götterdämmerung," the Emperor renounced all claims to divinity. The military stood disarmed. For the first time in her long history Japan had foreign troops on her soil. For a proud people this was "to suffer the insufferable.

"Obviously many of the Japanese felt that they had been deceived. All of their religious sentiments had been channeled into one great bloody river of sacrifice for the Emperor and for *Dai Nippon*. Now they had lost all. They had been betrayed even by their own religion. If there was anything at all to religion maybe it could be found in the religion of the conqueror."

So people of every class turned to Christianity, seeking consolation. The conversion rate during the years immediately after the war has never been equalled in modern Japan.

Misfortune makes people turn to something higher in search of relief. Yet when things improve the attention of the supplicant quickly descends to things of the world. That is what happened in Japan.

Ironically, it was another war, the one that started in Korea in June of 1950, that brought the Japanese back from spiritual interests to materialistic desires. When Americans once more became involved in combat in Asia they did not have to depend completely on the manufacture and repair of weapons in the United States, not with the industrial potential and the diligent people of Japan less than an hour's plane trip from Korea.

The factories, silent since the World War, rumbled into action overnight. At the urging of the United States, Japan began to thrive. Suddenly she became a major power in the markets of the world. Standards of living soared. Through their own efforts the people lifted themselves out of despondency. Japan was back. She had a national purpose. Her conqueror had become her ally!

This is remembered as the "Korean boom." It was followed by the "Vietnam boom."

Father Horgan recalled: "Results were quick and visible—my house, my car, my television set. If religion wanted to compete it would have to produce such visible results. Material pressures dispel thoughts of religion. Soon the ideal becomes *za guddo raifu*, the good life. When the good times come they bring with them few brakes, either moral or economic."

Father Horgan is aware of the various theories as to how the Japanese character causes Christianity to make slow progress here. Some say that the Japanese find partial religious satisfaction in an almost ritualistic observance of all rules of courtesy. Anyone attending a formal tea ceremony may sense some validity in this.

Other observers believe that the Japanese have such a preoccupation with the beauties of nature that it must be an expression of their religious instinct. They hold Mount Fuji in almost mystic awe. And a family in the darkest slum will spend long hours decorating the house with exquisite flower arrangements. No doubt there is some religious reverence reflected in this sense of beauty.

Another reason given for the people's indifference to Christianity is that the Japanese are opposed to foreign things. This is certainly not apparent in cities where foreign goods and customs are imitated to an unfortunate degree. Nevertheless there is still marked antiforeign feeling in the traditionally conservative areas in Kyushu and central Honshu, especially in the countryside. The impact on the rural population has been almost nil, except for a few exceptions. Perhaps this can be attributed to the conservatism of country people one meets all over the world.

And yet, observed Father Horgan, Christians are well regarded in Japan and tend to have an influence beyong their numbers. They are of such quality that they have enriched Christianity spiritually and culturally. Their numbers are not likely to grow quickly, at least not in the near future. However, there will be a steady trickle of converts as long as the government is friendly and missionaries are free to go about their work.

"I do not believe in mass conversions," said Father Horgan with feeling. "They are notoriously ephemeral. Among an educated people you will never have mass acceptance of any religion.

"The rate of conversions to Catholicism in Japan is the same as the rate in Britain. Japan will never become a land one hundred percent Christian, but there will always be a strong Christianity here. Call Christians an elite.

"The spread of Christianity is not up to the missionary, but to the Spirit and the Japanese. A missionary is merely an instrument of the Spirit. The old-time missionary used to think that he was more influential than he was.

"It is not 'the excellence of the doctrine' that moves people to the Church. What moves them is the Spirit, and that is a mystery. The influence that the missionary has depends on the life that he lives. It is not the words he preaches but the life he lives that has the first effect.

"People must first say, 'We would like to know what makes this man tick.' Then they are ready for the doctrine."

I thought that the metal cylinder inside the front door of the rectory at Ryujin was an umbrella stand. Father Horgan told me it came from a United States Air Corps bomber that crashed near here in 1945, three months before the end of the war. Many stories have grown up around the crash and what happened afterward. Before they all blend into a blurred legend, Father Horgan is separating fact from fiction and putting it down on paper.

Even though the crash was on May 5, the day of Boys' Festival, no children had hung paper carps on bamboo poles for fear that the bright colors might make it easier for American pilots to spot occupied places. Yet a party ought to be safe enough, and so Toshi Ikeda, seventeen, and her younger brothers, Tsuneji and Takashi, were preparing one with a frugal menu.

Suddenly a siren moaned through Ryujin valley. A low-flying B-29 came over with a roar. A thunderous explosion shattered the windows of the house. The Ikedas ran outside in time to see a blazing bomber overhead. Two parachutes drifted by and disappeared over the mountain.

Within moments the speaker system came alive. It was connected with the local Civil Defense headquarters: "Get your bamboo spears and shields. Assemble at Tonohara (four miles away). Enemy aircraft has fallen.

Armed men have parachuted. This is no drill. This is no drill, on the double!''

Through research Father Horgan has learned why the bomber happened to be where it was on that fateful morning in May. When a fog turned soupy and a compass went haywire, Captain McPherson's B-29 became lost enroute to the target, Kure Port in Hiroshima Prefecture. Fuel that was to get the plane back to Saipan was used circling the comparatively safe Wakayama mountains, trying to regain bearings and re-establish contact with other B-29s.

Captain McPherson hesitated to drop bombs, even in this remote area, for fear of attracting attention. He even skimmed dangerously low over mountains hoping to evade radar.

His efforts were in vain. Suddenly two *Hayabushi* (Falcon) interceptors darted out of the morning sun with guns blazing. The bomber's mid-section loaded with three tons of incendiaries, burst into an inferno.

Captain McPherson and his flight engineer, Lawrence Parker, left the plane together and reached earth safely. Six others who had survived the fire died either from faulty parachutes or from burns. The explosion, which had shattered the Ikedas' windows, fragmented the plane's tail section even before the parachutes had reached the ground.

Father Horgan's story now shifts to Shoichi Adachi, eighteen, and his brother Teizo. They had wanted to go into battle to die for the Emperor, but were denied that dubious honor. Their father, a swordmaker, was in poor health and so his sons had to stay at home to help provide anachronistic weapons—the sabers which Japanese officers still carried as a badge of rank.

Because he had three months of basic military training Shoichi Adachi was now a corporal in charge of the home guard at Tonohara. Those frightening orders coming over the speaker system sent him and his brother running to the place of assembly, the school yard in Tonohara, carrying helmets, rifles, and bayonets.

Shoichi Adachi told Father Horgan that he recalls how he felt when he saw two parachutes floating into the mountains. Propaganda and privations had prepared him for this. His finger itched on the trigger.

After a two-hour search the Adachis and three other young men found the two Americans sitting on the ground outside a charcoal-burner's hut. Their parachutes were neatly folded and their side arms were on the ground in front of them.

First he must interrogate the two Americans. He ordered them to turn their pockets inside out. That did it!

"Perhaps it was the pathetic humanness of the contents," said Father Horgan. "Some bitter green plums, a few heads of unripe barley, a pamphlet telling how to survive if shot down, and a small Bible. Something melted inside Corporal Adachi. He saw two human beings instead of two enemy soldiers. He no longer wanted to kill them."

Members of the home guard tied the captives' hands and marched them down a narrow river towards Tonohara. The villagers with their bamboo spears converged on Adachi and his prisoners. About a hundred milled around out of curiosity. They, too, had seen propaganda posters and films depicting Americans as rude, hairy savages, but here stood two helpless young men, about twenty years old. The villagers of Tonohara still wonder at their own lack of hostility.

The Americans had also been subjected to propaganda. When Mrs. Yasu Fukase offered them some boiled rice they did not accept it, perhaps fearing it was poisoned. They did, however, accept cigarettes from Mrs. Raku Yamamoto, owner of the tobacco shop.

"Meanwhile, the search for the fallen B-29 and the remaining crew members continued," said Father Horgan. "In the valley of Ongyoji, the main section of the downed plane had sliced a swath through a cedar forest and lay remarkably intact astride the small river. The fuselage contained the charred remains of those killed in the fighter attack. The bodies of two others who had parachuted hung tangled in a tree. The stream was discolored by spilled fuel. Toshi Ikeda still remembers the rainbow colors of the scum and the white bellies of the perch floating dead on the surface."

At dark the two Americans were kept under guard in a shed. Adachi remembers how they prayed before retiring and how well they slept.

He himself did not sleep. War seemed unglamorous now. He is not ashamed to admit that he cried that night.

When word of the crash reached Regional Headquarters the dreaded *Kempei*, military police, hurried by motorcycle from Wakayama City to Ryujin and on to Tonohara. When they took charge of the prisoners the gentleness of the mountain folk no longer prevailed. The *Kempei* manhandled the Americans, tied them up roughly and shoved them into the sidecars. An old woodsman tried to intercede and was beaten.

The Americans tried to thank the villagers, but sharp blows cut short their farewell. The military police pointed to the captives and said, "Here is the enemy! Here are the foreign devils who would destroy Japan and His Imperial Majesty!"

The mountain people called to the captives, "*Sayonara, Ki wo tsukete.*" "Goodbye and take care."

Father Horgan has never been able to document the fate of the Americans. "Dark rumors, never confirmed, have occasionally surfaced about their treatment by angry rabble in another town. Some say they were taken to Kobe and executed. All that we know for certain is that they did not survive the war."

Back in Tonohara, Corporal Adachi and his brother took charge of assembling the remains of the dead crewmen. Those that they found they wrapped in parachutes and buried. At ceremony, a Buddhist *bonze* chanted the O-Kyo, the *sutras* that mourn the dead.

Within days after the war's end American soldiers arrived in Tonohara to exhume the remains and send them first to Yokahama's cemetery for foreigners and later to the United States for military honors.

Salvaged sections of the bomber fetched good prices when sold as scrap metal. The charred scar in the mountains turned green again. Only a wooden cross marked the site of the burial place.

"As woodsmen and farmers passed the cross they stopped and prayed for their former enemies," said Father Horgan. "Daily, without fail, local ladies placed flowers in the bamboo vases that flanked the cross. Someone suggested a more permanent monument and the idea caught on. From their meager incomes, the villagers collected several thousand dollars."

On December 12, 1947, a six-foot stone of local black granite replaced the wooden cross. On the face of the stone, under the carved outline of a cross, are Chinese characters which say, "In memory of the American officers and men of the Allied Forces who died in War." Underneath, in English, is the message, "Where love is, God is."

"The little 'Sacred Book' that the Americans carried is now well known in these parts," said Father Horgan. "In Ryujin a Catholic church was founded in 1948, across the mountain from the village of Tonohara. Their preschool children learn about the God of Love in the Catholic nursery school across from Mrs. Yamamoto's tobacco shop. Some of their daughters received their First Communion in silk dresses that were cut from parachutes which Toshi Ikeda, a Christian, managed to hide before the *Kempei* could lay hands on them.

"Each May 5 a Buddhist *bonze* and a Catholic priest join the villagers at the granite monument to offer services for the dead and pray for world peace."

May 1
Sunday

While walking through the misty valley at dawn I could see why NHK-TV did a documentary film here. The well-proportioned little cream-colored church, with its freestanding bell tower sits in a valley surrounded on three sides by green mountains. The tranquility appealed to the producer.

"In the film they wanted a baptism, a marriage, and a funeral," said Father Alec Eaton, the pastor in Ryujin in those days. "I said I could provide a baptism and a marriage, but I would not kill for a funeral. The baby cried at the pouring of the water, so the NHK boys were delighted—it was just what they wanted."

The director had Father Eaton ride his bike twice across an icy suspension bridge that wobbles. Three "takes" were needed on the frigid day he rode along a snow-covered mountain road. The biggest hit in the film was the scene in which kindergarten kids pushed their pastor on a playground swing.

The documentary, shown in prime time, had an estimated audience of twenty million. One minute after the show went off the air, at eight o'clock in the evening, the phone in the rectory began ringing as calls came in from all over the country for the next few days. Then letters began coming. After that visitors arrived. People at the far end of the parish, twenty miles away, were asked nearly every day, "Where is that church?"

"The show was so well done," said Father Eaton, "that many outsiders got the impression that the whole place was Catholic and a wonderful spirit existed there. I was coming in to lunch one day when I met a young man of twenty-one, weighed down with several bags. I invited him in. He said, 'I have permission from my family to come and live with you. I am from Tokyo and I don't like the life up there. When I saw the TV I said that is the place for me.'

"I gave him lunch and then got some Catholic men to talk with him and explain things. One of them said he would put him up for the night. The guest stayed a week.

"Next came a Korean girl, born in Japan, who had suffered a lot as a student. She tried suicide but failed. My housekeeper put her up in her own room for three days and fed her. She went back to Osaka, went to the nearest church, took instructions and was baptized.

"A 25-year-old Catholic man from Tokyo came to stay one night and stayed a week. Calls kept coming from people asking if they could stay at the church. Luckily most of the calls came to the kindergarten and the teachers knew how to refuse without losing face."

The letters were full of questions: "How do we get there?" "Give us some details about the village."

Priests are allowed to perform pagan weddings in the church. These grew in number after the television documentary. One couple wanted to get away from friends because the reception costs too much. The next also had financial problems, but they brought twenty friends with them. The third bride said she had a dream seven years ago in which she was promised a wedding in a quiet country place. From being a performer in a film, Father Eaton learned the power of television.

Also while walking through the valley this morning I kept remembering that the thing Father Flinn disliked about Ryujin was snakes. He always dreaded September because that is when they are everywhere. He shrank from leaving the church grounds. Snakes prefer paddy fields, and water, and tall grass, and he feared they might prefer him, too.

One day, on a hike with altar boys, he nearly stepped on a snake. After jumping high and yelling, he was startled to see the boys take off after the snake. They explained, "Father, we can get fifty yen for a snake."

September is especially the month of the *mamushi*. It is not a snake but an adder. (A snake lays eggs; an adder carries its young in its womb and emits them from its mouth.)

The *mamushi*, Japan's only poisonous serpent, measures from eighteen inches to two feet. Each year it kills about twenty-five people and causes extreme discomfort to about four hundred.

The adder, dark brown or black, has an irregular pattern of blotches on its back. Its underside is light tan or grey, and spotted with dark markings. The head is diamond-shaped and thick.

When Father Flinn's friend, Yanagawa San, encountered a *mamushi* he described the event in some detail.

"Father, you see it was like this. I went out to catch this *mamushi*, but he caught me."

Tears of laughter rolled down his cheeks as he held up his swollen and badly discolored leg.

"I was stupid to go after him without any shoes on. He got me here. See the two fang marks. Kochan, my son, sucked at the punctures. My foot swelled up and turned purple. Did it hurt! Cold sweat all over me. Cramps in my chest. They put a tourniquet on my leg and sent me to the doctor. No antidote available. A car relay brought some from Tanabe hospital. I got the injection three and a half hours after the bite. The leg was swollen to the knee. Sure I was scared."

He had caught the *mamushi* and that consoled him somewhat for all the pain.

Apart from the *mamushi* the Japanese have no great fear of snakes. White snakes live in the roofs and under the floors of homes. These six-foot creatures are supposed to bring prosperity and good luck.

Father Flinn said that when Father Kevin Lynch killed a huge snake in front of his church he felt sure he had done the community a service. On the contrary, he was asked to pay compensation to the disconsolate family whose pet he had destroyed.

Each year about five million snakes are consumed as food or medicine in Japan. The demand is increasing. In Tokyo alone there are sixty-five licensed dealers who employ professional catchers.

Ikeda Tsuneji San, a young worker on a lumber gang makes a good living on the side catching adders. Some days he bags four or five, spearing them through the head with a sharp, wood pike.

Families keep an adder's body pickled in alcohol for medicinal purposes. Powdered snake is found in the first aid kits in homes.

Father Flinn said: "Why not try some snake pills next time you're not feeling well? When you have a temperature, just slip a bit of dried snake into water, bring it to a boil and drink. If your throat is sore or inflamed, a gargle of the same mixture, will work wonders. Festered finger? Nothing to beat a tight bandage of snake skin. Feeling tired or run down? A good dose of snake should perk you up. Mental energy is improved, muscular strength developed, and physical well-being is assured to those who take snake hormones regularly as a tonic. Athletes, judo wrestlers, and marathon runners in Japan are among the snake addicts."

Father Flinn asked doctors in the village if they really thought snake medicine has any value. They were slow to rule it out.

One September he decided to get away from the snakes. He wrote to Father Barry Cairns in Tokyo saying he would like to come to the city for a few days.

"Come by all means," Father Cairns wrote back. "I've just found an exciting restaurant. At Iwasaki's Eating Palace, besides fried ants, roasted praying mantises, baked dragon flies and bullfrogs, you can order snake steaks. And for drinks you have a choice: minced snake meat in fruit juice or wine. Let's try it!"

At Mass forty-six parishioners greeted their old pastor with affection. There was a great to-do of deep bows, handshakes, slaps on the shoulder, and hugs. Japanese are given to standing outside the church and chatting following the service.

Shortly after Mass Father Flinn and I took a bus from Ryujin to the railroad station at Tanabe. If the driver seems especially skillful, Father explained, it is because the bus company refuses to hire anyone who has not had at least five years of experience handling heavy logging trucks as they careen down these mountain roads.

Yesterday, all the way up the mountain, Father commented on how improved this road is since he lived here from 1954 until 1972. Today, on the way down, he made the same observation, perhaps hoping to assuage my fears.

He came to know the old road well because he and Father Leo Baker were called upon often to use the parish car as an ambulance. In those days Ryujin was no place to be taken suddenly ill or be seriously injured in an accident. There were doctors, but no hospital, no surgery, and no ambulance. The bus stopped at 6 P.M., but even a bus ride to the nearest hospital in Tanabe, on the coast, was a three-hour ordeal of endurance over rough and dangerous roads.

So people asked the priests to take sick and injured to the hospital in the parish car. Generally, they did not ask unless the need was real.

Most of the patients were woodcutters hurt by sliding logs or rolling rocks. Sometimes there were acute cases of appendicitis. Occasionally truck drivers were injured in a plunge off the road over a cliff, but that was not too often because the roads were so dangerous that the drivers were particularly careful.

Now and again the trip to the hospital was a race against the clock. It was that way the day Father Baker drove Mrs. Hatamura, the mother of seven children, who suffered from cancer. She hemorrhaged badly on the way and collapsed unconscious upon arrival in Tanabe. Nurses picked her up from the ground and rushed her straight to the theatre for an emergency operation.

In time she was fit and strong and could hold her own among the other local women who carried baskets of stones to men mixing concrete.

One day, when Father Baker met Mrs. Hatamura working hard at her job, she beamed and said, "Today is the first anniversary, Father."

"Of what?" he asked.

"Of the day the priest's car saved my life."

In Japan the booklets and the posters which promote holidays usually feature pictures of flower-filled fields, calm lakes, noble mountains. No people. No houses. No automobiles. The big cities have an oversupply of those. No wonder people are attracted to Ryujin even with its tortuous roads and snakes.

Now we are returning to Wakayama City and from there will go on to other cities. Our country visits are about over. There will be less time for long rambling conversations, the kind Father Horgan and I had by the fire last night.

May 2
Monday

When Father Flinn and I returned to Wakayama City, Miss Inagaki served spaghetti, and very good spaghetti indeed. I have a hunch that she asked Father to name one of my favorite dishes.

Miss Inagaki has been housekeeper in this parish for thirty-three years. Soon she will retire, but will remain here living in her apartment. The pastor is building a house for her successor.

This morning I saw a good example of the thoughtfulness that Columbans show for their housekeepers. Father Flinn went to the cemetery to say Mass at the grave of his former housekeeper, Sogawa Komitsu San, and took with him her daughters, Takako and Setsuko, and their husbands.

Father recalled that privations of war undermined Sogawa Komitsu's health. Although ill, and living in primitive conditions with insufficient food, she took very good care of her two small daughters. Her husband returned from the war a sick man and died soon after.

"From the day of her baptism she came alive with a new energy," said Father Flinn. "When the church in Ryujin was in need of help she offered to be housekeeper for Father Brian Gallagher and myself. She did more than those chores. She visited the sick and filled in as kindergarten teacher when needed.

"She diligently prepared classes in Christian doctrine and conducted them each Sunday. I frequently told her to forget the books and share her own experiences of God with the children."

Father Flinn observed that in the history of the Japanese church, dating back to almost four hundred years, there are many martyrs. Over two hun-

91

dred have either been canonized or beatified and of this number more than thirty are listed as "housekeepers." Some died on crosses in Osaka, others were buried alive, burned alive, or beheaded in Nagasaki.

"Today the housekeepers in Japan are not called on to serve Christ in 'dungeon, fire and sword'," said Father Flinn, "though they may occasionally suffer by having to keep house for foreigners who think, feel, and speak so differently from them."

During his early years the closest contact a missionary has with the culture and life of the Japanese is through his housekeeper. She is the contact with the community at large. She deals with the police, interviews beggars, controls peddlers, the postman, and delivery and service men. She answers the phone. She reads the local news in the papers, or at least the words that the priest cannot puzzle out. She dashes off each morning to mix with the local women at the little shops. She is a genius at being able to work out what day to go where for the choicest and cheapest fish, fruit, and vegetables.

Father Flinn said that he and a good many other missionaries in Japan are willing to admit that they would have been hindered in their work had it not been for a devoted band of housekeepers.

Father John Burger, a Columban from the United States, took me for a walk around the shopping district of Wakayama City.

"What do you like least about Japan?" he asked.

"The crowds."

"I know what you mean," he said. "When first I came here I used to say to myself, on every trip, 'I certainly picked a bad day to travel.' Soon I realized that in Japan every day is a bad day to travel."

"What do you like best about the Japanese?" he asked.

"Their personal discipline."

We stopped at several galleries that exhibit *sumi-e*, the most disciplined of all art forms. With varying shades of black ink on white paper or silk, the artist creates a world that is usually sombre without being depressing.

Sumi-e demands more control that oil painting. Working with oils on canvas the artist can cover a mistake and make adjustments freely. The *sumi-e* artist must get it right the first time because black ink permeates the paper and silk fabric.

Such ink paintings were being produced in China more than a thousand years ago. They were started in Japan when Zen priests began painting with ink as a hobby. It fit their philosophy. They believe in a simple, frugal life without ostentation; so a monochromatic aesthetic suits their inclinations.

When I said that what I like best about Japanese is their personal discipline, I meant more than the disciplined beauty of their art. To explain in more detail, I had better wait until near the end of this trip.

A dozen parishioners from Holy Family church, in that part of Wakayama City known as Imafuka, took Father Sean Corr, their pastor, and Father Flinn and me to dinner. The occasion was in honor of Father Flinn, the pastor of their church from 1972 until 1978.

Most restaurants in Japan have *Shokuhin Sanpuru* in a glass case near the front door, but the one we went to tonight is too elegant for that. (*Shokuhin Sanpuru* is artificial food; you might call it a vinyl plastic menu. The models, highly colored, sometimes look remarkably real.)

We were led by the *Jochu-san*, the honorable Miss Waitress, to a room set off from the rest by screens of amber paper. Since the *shoji* screens separated us from other diners and the *tatami* mats and low table were of such simplicity, the room was truly "furnished with guests."

At the sight of *tatami* I flinched for that means we will be sitting on the floor. Not even in youth was I able to tuck my legs under in the approved way, and so I sprawl in a most ungainly manner. After seeing me lean against a post, a waitress brought me a back rest, a seat with a back to it, a chair without legs.

The quality of the *tatami* is said to reflect the status of a Japanese home. The elegance of the restaurant is also reflected in the excellence of the *tatami*. The skill of the craftsman is apparent in how he sews the ornamental cloth borders so that all edges are straight and even. Well-made mats show no space between sections. The main bulk of the *tatami* is rice straw compressed and trimmed to form a mat six feet by three feet and three inches thick. An outer cover, woven from reed, is sewn over the surface to give a smooth finish. Rice straw is especially suited to Japan's weather. While carpets get soggy in summer, straw absorbs moisture leaving the outside of the mat crisp and dry. In winter the thick mat is an excellent insulator.

After we were seated, a waitress in snow-white socks entered quietly. With a light gliding motion she swooped downward, coming to a soft poised rest on her knees at the edge of the table.

In front of us she placed hot *sake* and cold beer. *Sake*, like Scotch, is an acquired taste. Someone described it as tasting like warm watered sherry; I find it similar to gin. Sake is *san*, honorable, which beer is not. Yet the Japanese make mighty good beer; they learned from the Germans and have surpassed their master.

We began with a bowl of simple clear soup. If there are speeches at a Japanese dinner, they come just after the soup or not at all. Father Flinn made a brief one explaining that we were on this journey so that I might tell the story of the Columban Fathers in Japan.

Among the exotic food that followed was *sashimi*, a tidbit prepared with raw, fresh fish. Any kind of fish will do, even shark or whale, but carp, bonito, tuna, and sea-bream are most suitable. The fish is sliced or cut into cubes, according to the kind that is used. The manner of cutting is important, for raw fish cut by an inexperienced hand loses all its flavor. The expert is familiar with several ways of slicing and each way has its effect on the flavor of *sashimi*.

Strips or cubes of fish are artfully arranged on special *sashimi* dishes. Again it takes an expert to make the precise arrangement which will whet the appetite. Color in the design comes from garnishes of sliced carrot, seaweed, cucumbers, radishes, chrysanthemums. Boiled chrysanthemums are often served as a side dish. (The recipe: boil the heads until they are soft; let stand for three hours and squeeze thoroughly; serve with sugar and vinegar according to taste.)

So that the design of the food could be seen from its best angle, the waitress rotated each plate as she set it down before us.

I was invited to walk through the kitchen. It is vast and furnished with utmost simplicity. No clutter. Nothing in sight that is not immediately in use. Although this is not a busy evening, the chefs seemed to concentrate on their work and were not distracting each other with chatter.

This brought to mind something a Buddhist abbess wrote about cooking, something she had learned from the founder of a Zen sect: "When washing rice, focus attention on the washing and let no distraction enter." She is convinced that this spiritual attitude toward cooking—"being totally present in what you are doing and allowing no distractions"—is valid anywhere in the world and that its application will bring any cooking to perfection.

(The Japanese tradition of doing things with attention shows up even in the way cab drivers and taxi drivers seem to concentrate on their work. Sometimes such attention can be maddening, for example, when you are standing in a long line at the airport waiting for passport control to inspect each document with what seems undue care.)

Japanese tend to be quiet at dinner, preferring to focus attention on the taste of the food. Not so tonight. Maybe they felt that the presence of an Australian, an Irishman, and an American requires chatter. So the kind of conversation at which the Japanese excel bubbled all around us.

I had once been told that if the conversation lags at a dinner party in Japan, just bring up the subject of proverbs. The Japanese enjoy talking about old sayings and comparing them with those of other countries. They like to tell of the occasion when they first heard a particular proverb—perhaps from mother or grandfather—and of the many times they saw this saying come true.

Here are a half dozen:

A wife and a cooking pot get better as they get older.

Cows herd with cows; horses with horses.

Erect a fence even between intimates.

It is better to go to heaven in rags than to hell in embroidery.

If you want to cure yourself of drunkenness, observe a drunkard when you are sober.

Dance when everybody else is dancing.

Thank goodness my ability to eat with chopsticks returned suddenly at the start of dinner tonight. A few days ago I tried using them and found that the knack had slipped away. Until tonight I was able to avoid them because we ate either in rectories or in restaurants that serve western food.

How do you manage with a bowl of soup and chopsticks? You sip the soup from the round deep bowl and use the chopsticks to lift out bits of meat, fish, or vegetable. Soup and noodles are slurped. If you do not slurp soup and noodles or green tea, you are considered odd.

"You can't enjoy Japanese food properly unless you learn the art of using chopsticks," Father Flinn told me the other day when I was being awkward with a pair. "Chopsticks to the Japanese are an extension of the thumb and first finger. Notice how food is served in small pieces. Slicing fish and meat into small pieces is a task for the cook alone. To show a knife is barbarous."

So that I might not do anything gauche he told of the taboos in the use of chopsticks:

Never use them as a toothpick.

Never hold them "on the ready" when asking for another bowl of rice, but place them on the "rest" provided.

Never let them hover over the many dishes placed before you; if you do it means than you are so greedy that the chopsticks "lose their way."

Never use them in the left hand. Father said that a lefthanded person, as he himself is, would do better to ask for a spoon than to make that mistake. He explained that bones at the crematorium are always handled with chopsticks held in the left hand.

Never put chopsticks farther than an inch into your mouth.

Never select anything from a dish that is being handed around with chopsticks that have been in your mouth. Use the serving chopsticks or turn your own around and use the other end.

Of course the Japanese have sayings in which chopsticks play a part. Of a penniless beggar they say, "He hasn't even any chopsticks," and of a rich person, "Her hands have never held anything heavier than a chopstick."

"Westerners never admire a foreigner who masters the art of using a knife and fork," said Father Flinn, "but Japanese are open in their admiration of a foreigner who masters the art of using chopsticks. Immediately they presume that he can read and write Japanese. And speak it. So they start talking to him in Japanese at a fast speed."

Nobody presumed that at the dinner party tonight. They saw at a glance that anyone sprawling in such an ungainly position on the *tatami*, who slurps soup in such a styleless way, and who clasps chopsticks in so clumsy a manner is too unsophisticated to speak the language. So all conversation between us had to pass back and forth, with their pastor, Father Sean Corr, as interpreter.

The restaurant has an *ofuro* that diners might use before, during, or after a meal. It looked like a small swimming pool with a haze of steam hanging over it, a scene out of Dante. I could not face up to that cauldron; you have to get used to such temperatures early in life.

The hot bath, *ofuro*, is a tradition here. Every Japanese family, every evening, takes its hot bath. One tubful of water serves the whole family, with members bathing in order of seniority.

A guest is supposed to go first. The guest cannot do anything to moderate the heat without interfering with the rights and comfort of those who follow. The entire supply of hot water in the house may be in that one tub.

Since the guest cannot refuse to bathe, without giving offense to the host, many a Columban missionary literally sweated out the *ofuro*. It simply won't do to go into the room, make splashing sounds, sprinkle a little water here and there, and come out saying how much you enjoyed yourself. If you have been in up to 120 degrees Fahrenheit, you emerge showing it, and there is no way of faking that look.

When a missionary was invited to use the *ofuro*, he accepted out of respect to Saint Paul's admonition to be all things to all men. He dipped a toe in the water, hastily withdrew it, looked Saint Paul in the eye and said: "Paul, that's fine as a principle, and I'm for it within reason, but even you must have reneged once in a while."

He came out making some lame excuse that did not even convince himself. The next in line was another Columban. He had studied physics and knowing that the hottest water rises to the top he stirred to get a more tolerable temperature throughout the tub.

On their way home the two missionaries tried to say something in favor of a scalding bath. They decided that the *ofuro* keeps the Japanese from getting backaches and rheumatism after working bent over all day in a chilly, flooded rice paddy.

I doubt that anyone in that elegant restaurant this evening is in danger of getting rheumatism from working in a flooded rice paddy.

May 3
Tuesday

We left Wakayama City early so that we might spend a few hours in Kyoto before going on to Tokyo.

On the train, a little girl clutched a plastic bag that held water and three goldfish. Maybe she has been charmed by the cry, "*Kingyo!*"

With the cry, "*Kingyo, kingyo!*" the goldfish-man comes pushing a bright wagon down the street. The magic in the sound causes children to gather in a hurry. The fishing begins.

For a few *yen* the goldfish-man supplies a tissue net. You may fish as long as the paper net lasts and take home whatever you catch. Lacking adeptness you might need several nets to catch a fish, but having the knack, you may get as many as five before the net dissolves.

Japanese children take good care of their goldfish, feeding them rice and crushed silkworm cocoons. Often they are kept in a pool in a small garden surrounded by dwarf trees, miniature shrines, and bridges.

Father Barry Cairns, an Australian Columban who recently returned to Japan, seems to know a great deal about goldfish. They arrived here from China in the seventeeth century, he says. Early varieties were small with insignificant tails, but the Japanese experimented to improve them. Dutch traders imported new varieties a hundred years after the Chinese. Gorgeous tropical species came in from Hawaii and the Ryukyu islands early this century. Fish fanciers experimented with cross breeding to produce bulging eyes, long waving tails and balloon-like bodies.

Rearing goldfish is a specialty of many small towns. What seems from a distance to be a flooded rice paddy turns out to be a flashing pool of gold.

We will pass near Koriyama this afternoon where six hundred acres are dedicated to raising goldfish.

This country produces seventy-five million fish annually, but only a half million are exported. The Japanese buy the rest; often with the cry of "*Kingyo, kingyo!*" ringing in their ears.

Up until now most travelers seemed to be young people on the move in groups. Today, maybe because it is Constitution Day, many families are up and about.

Family life is still strong in village and countryside, Father Flinn tells me. The family's chief concern is to do its duty toward ancestors and to hand down the family name and property through marriage. Such interests come before those of the individual.

Like the family, the village community is a tightly knit unit. Planting and harvesting are done in common. Neighbors within a hamlet work together until everyone's crops are sown and gathered. Many festivals follow the agricultural calendar.

Rejoicing is also done in common as neighbors gather for drinking *shochu*, singing, and dancing. At national festivals everyone repairs to the local temple or shrine to participate in a ceremony. Often the temple grounds are enlivened by wrestling matches and fairs.

Such togetherness, Father Flinn observed, makes it difficult for an individual to become a Christian. Anyone who breaks away from full unity with the group is branded as a *henjin*, a strange person.

When we saw a group of people coming from a funeral, Father Flinn said that the Japanese attitude toward death always fascinates him; it is different from ours. He has seen many Japanese die and has made the funeral arrangements for an even greater number. Theirs is not the same as the Western approach to death as described by Dr. Elisabeth Kübler-Ross.

Dr. Kübler-Ross observed the dying pass through five emotional stages:

Denial—"I don't believe it. It can't be true. I'll get another doctor . . . go to a famous clinic."

Anger—"Why me? Why should it be me? It's unjust."

Bargaining—"Look, God, I'll live a much better life if you'll only work a miracle and let me live."

Depression—"I must leave all of these things, all my loved ones. It's the end for me."

Acceptance—"Well, my time has come. I'm going to die. That's how it is."

"Your attitude toward death is based on what you believe death to be and what will happen after that," said Father Flinn. "My Japanese friends do not think they pass through the same emotional stages as Westerners. They do not fear death; they accept it as part of life.

"I have met many old people in country areas who hoped for death because after a long and active life they could no longer produce anything to add to the family's income. Rather than be a burden, they prefer to die. In that way they will become a respected ancestor, a protector, and a benefactor of the family."

This attitude comes down from the distant past. Japanese believed that death does not take them apart from the land of the living. They will dwell in a tomb instead of a house, but through supernatural powers make the family happy if the family is good to them and cause plenty of trouble if neglected. So they were reasonably sure that the family would show them respect by daily offerings of food and drink.

At a later date the Japanese came to believe that the spirits of the dead control the happenings of earth—seasons, harvests, pestilence, famine, typhoons, and earthquakes. So they had a fear of the deceased and were much concerned about all the rites due to them.

Although Confucianism and later Buddhism freed the Japanese from such oppressive fear, the basic ideas have persisted. The household shrine—the *mitamaya* or god shelf of the Shinto rite, and the *butsudan*, family altar, of Buddhism—is still the center of Japanese home life. Each holds tablets inscribed with the names of ancestors. Each day members of the household offer prayers and food. This simple gesture may take only a couple of minutes but must never be omitted.

Most Japanese seem to think that one's belief during life determines how the soul will be disposed of after death. A Shinto soul will hover about the village shrine; a Shinshu Buddhist will go to Amida's heaven; and a Zen Buddhist will enjoy some other heaven. Many believe that after death they are gathered into Buddha's lap and become buddhas themselves.

Some do not fear death because they will go from one good place to another. Death is an extension of this life rather than an end of it. Some Japanese, however, believe that they will return to Mu, nothingness.

"There are so many discrepancies in the Japanese outlook," said Father Flinn. Some fear death; others do not. Death is a forbidden word in certain circumstances. The very hint of it on a joyous occasion is frowned upon. And taboos about death are abundant. The most obvious to visitors is the absence of fourth floors in hospitals and in many hotels. The word for four and the word for death have the same pronunciation—*shee*.

100

With a fatalistic expression the Japanese usually shrug off any depressing mood connected with death: "*Shigata-ga-nai.*" "It can't be avoided. Nothing can be done about it. It can't be helped."

When I see Japanese laughing I am often reminded that a young missionary is not here long before he is puzzled by some of the laughter.

For example, when a Catholic woman called on a priest she was smiling as though she had dropped by for a casual visit. In the sitting room she laughingly apologized for disturbing him at such an early hour. She broke into still louder laughter and in what seemed a cheerful manner told the priest why she had come. Her son was killed two days ago while working in the mountains. He had been crushed by a falling tree. Only then did the missionary notice how desperately her hands were clasping and unclasping the handkerchief in her lap, and how her whole body was shaking in an agony of grief.

While traveling by train, a Columban met a man from Hiroshima. The talk turned to the atomic bombing of that city and its terrible effects. The man from Hiroshima described the charred and mangled bodies in gruesome detail, but with what seemed a cheerful relish. The more macabre the details the more he roared with merriment. The priest realized that this laughter was covering embarrassment, revulsion, and disgust.

The Japanese do cry on occasion. A photograph of a crowd cheering the Emperor shows a tear on the cheek of an old woman. Japanese athletes often break into tears when they lose. Politicians sometimes cry when delivering a speech. At the theatre men and women weep openly.

But restraint is the ideal. The Japanese are masters in masking their emotions.

We had hoped to spend several hours in the heart of Kyoto just walking and gawking, but noise pollution has spoiled the morning. This is Constitution Day and the politicians are out in force.

Politics appeals to the Japanese. Seventy percent of the electorate turn out for local elections as compared with fifty percent in the United States.

Trucks with speaker's platforms atop them stand at nearly every street corner. Public address systems fill the air with penetrating decibels. People with axes to grind always spoil the environment.

Politicians call for rearmament or warn against it, promote Communism or condemn it, plead for a return to old ways or urge a rush to the new.

Here on Constitution Day the big question is whether or not Prime

Minister Yasuhiro Nakasone is "hawkish." One of the speakers said that the Japanese should be satisfied with the military shield that the United States has held over this country for nearly forty years. Because of it the Japanese have kept the defense budget under one percent of the GNP while the United States has been spending 6.3 percent of its GNP on the military.

In a survey taken two months ago, 72 percent of those polled disapproved of an increase in defense spending. Strangely enough, even though the opposition parties, the Socialists and the Communists, have also been against defense spending they have not attracted the majority of the voters.

This morning every political party is telling downtown Kyoto how wonderful it is. The Liberal Democratic Party and the Japan Socialist Party get the most votes, so they feel most smug. Some of the votes have been taken from them by the *Komeito*, or Clean Government Party, the political arm of the Soka Gakkai, a group with a philosophy based on a rigorous Buddhist sect, semi-military and highly political. In a tie for fourth place are the Socialist Party and the Communist Party.

Communism here has lost its Marxist base. Right after the war Marxism thrived in the universities, but the country's prodigious economic growth seems to have caused its decline until now there are few "pure Marxists" remaining. Old Marxist pragmatists have become liberals, even conservatives. Dyed-in-the-wool Communists find this dismaying because the old Marxists now form the right wing of the Socialist movement and are anti-Red to the core.

"If Communism has slipped it has not been because of a lack of propaganda," Father Flinn said. "Radio programs have been beamed from Moscow, Peking, Pyongyang, and Vladivostok. Communist reading matter is sold at low prices. A dozen Communist magazines sell for the price of one American publication. And there are many people willing to distribute Communist propaganda free. I remember when our local doctor used to urge patients to take from his waiting room the latest illustrated magazine from Peking."

Although Communists have not been getting the votes, they have won a victory of a kind. At the end of the Second World War, Father Patrick O'Connor, interviewed Sanzo Nosaka, the head of the Communist Party in Japan. Nosaka told the Columban, "We are materialists. Our goal is to make religion disappear." Their hope for a materialistic society has been fulfilled.

In the streets of Kyoto the sight of many flags—white with a large red sun—brought uncomfortable twinges. I had expected to feel such when meeting Japanese men of my own age, but felt none. The flags did it, though, suggesting the power of a symbol.

When I told a Columban that I feel no resentment toward Japanese veterans, he said they would feel none toward me, but that their parents might. People in their eighties and nineties who lost sons in the war still hate Americans. When hatred becomes a matter of conscience the old ones whisper it in the confessional.

I wonder if anyone ever shouts *"Banzai!"* (Hurrah for the Emperor!) In wartime that was a much publicized shout. (Later I learned that *Banzai* is still shouted on occasions of joy or victory.)

Someone told me that before the war when a bus or a train passed the Imperial Palace the conductor would say, "Deep reverence, everybody, please!" Passengers would stand and bow.

One thing about spending the morning of Constitution Day in Kyoto—it makes you aware of how fast things can change.

Money trays seem more prevalent here than any other place we have been. Maybe that is because all traditions linger in Kyoto. Samurai warriors were so disdainful of money that they would not touch it with their hands. I am told that is why money is often handed to you on a tray in banks and at the post office.

Many Japanese are afraid of what a great deal of money might do to them. Lottery prizes sometimes go unclaimed. One man refused to accept a hundred thousand dollars fearing it would ruin his relations with neighbors and friends who might resent his good fortune.

Kazue Uemura found a bag containing twenty-one gold bars worth nearly a half-million dollars. He turned it over to the police. When the gold was not claimed after a stipulated amount of time, it was offered to Kazue who renounced all claims to it explaining: "From the time I fished it up, I have been plagued by nasty phone calls asking what I am going to do with all that money. After consulting with my friends I have decided that I am better off without it."

This journey has often brought to mind one I took in 1944 traveling for eight days by train from Bombay in southwest India to Assam in the northeast. On the seventh day of that trip I realized that not once had I looked out of the window without seeing at least one human being.

The feeling of inundation by multitudes comes over me here, for Japan is the most densely populated major country in the world. I could never live here; the place is so steeped in human life that I could never come to terms with the intensity of it.

I have often said that everyone should spend at least one morning of his life in the Far East; the experience will leave a mark on the soul. Although Japan is in the Far East and has humanity galore it is not the place I recommend for that unique experience. It has a foot in two hemispheres—Asian by geography, race and heritage; Western in technology, ideas, laws, and institutions.

Take technology, for example. In day by day encounters with it, you get the feeling that the Japanese are more Western than the United States. This comes out in dozens of small ways: When taking a cab you never touch a door; it is opened and closed from the driver's seat. Windshield wipers are sensitive to the force of rain and so move faster as the downpour increases. On inter-island flights airplanes have screens up front so that the passengers can watch take-offs and landings as the pilot sees them. The blind have long had textured tiles in the sidewalk to guide them; added to this are birdcalls that tell how the stoplight is changing, and vibrating posts at intersections that also signal when it is safe to cross. And on and on.

The Shinkansen bullet train rushes between Kyoto and Tokyo in two hours and fifty minutes. A century ago fifty-three post stations along this route offered food and lodging to travelers on foot, in carriages, or on horseback.

I am collecting place names. Not far from a Columban church is the Street before the Temple-of-the-Happiness-to-Come. Others with religious associations are Nishi-no-Miya or Templewest and Miyashita, Below the Temple.

Many towns have names that when translated into English sound like something back home. Nishi-no-Hama is Westbeach; Nishizaki, West Point; Iwai, Rockwell; and Tateyama, Castlehill. Then there are Longbeach, Bamboohill, Pinehill, Five Wells, Looking-glass Bay, and Duck River.

The names of some towns have stories attached to them. Kisarazu loosely translated means "Our chief has come to stay." The legend is that years ago when warriors were making an approach by sea they found the going rough. The wife of the chief, the only woman on board, took for granted that she was bringing bad luck and so jumped overboard. The expedition was successful. The chief, loath to leave the place where his wife had given her life, decided to settle there. Hence the name: "Our chief has come to stay."

We have come to Tokyo, not to stay, but to catch our breath and collect clean clothes before taking off for Chiba Prefecture and Kanagawa Prefecture.

May 4
Wednesday

I was pleased at breakfast to have Father Gerald Griffin walk into the dining room here in the Columban Central House. I have been wanting to thank him for the useful maps he made and sent to me in the States.

When starting research for this trip, about a year ago, I wrote to the Central House asking for a map locating each of the missionaries in Japan and the thirty-nine Columban parishes. Father Griffin drew a fine set, showing the four prefectures in which Columbans work—Kumamoto, Wakayama, Chiba, and Kanagawa. (The latter two we must still visit.) These were helpful in getting ready for the trip and useful every day of it.

When I began talking about the work I have seen missionaries doing, Father Griffin recalled his days as a seminarian in County Meath, some thirty years ago, when he had a definite idea of what a missionary does. The lives of many missionaries today, he said, are far different from what he imagined them.

As a seminarian he had pictured himself in an undeveloped country existing in primitive conditions. He would be the "wise man" from the West, bravely living among the uneducated. In a remote, rural community he would be isolated from fellow missionaries and would see them only after traveling long distances by boat, horseback, or on foot.

He did not expect to be living among such cultivated, educated people as the contemporary Japanese. Certainly, he did not picture himself in a highly industrialized nation that has a gross national product ranking near the top. He did not foresee missionaries working in the largest city in the world with a transportation system unequaled anywhere.

What a difference a few years can make!

The chief of a primitive tribe once said: "You missionaries are good and kind people, but you are scratching where it doesn't itch."

When Father Griffin began feeling that he was scratching where it didn't itch, he got an idea of what to do about it. The seed for the idea was planted in 1967 when he was attending the East Asian Pastoral Institute in Manila. He realized that the traditional system of teaching about Christianity is inadequate if the people being taught are from a non-Christian culture.

This idea grew when he attended a course in counseling at Sophia, the Jesuit university in Tokyo, and as it ripened he decided to work toward a master's degree in counseling at Saint Paul's University in Ottawa, Canada.

"I realized that catechesis should begin with the needs of the individual and not begin immediately with theology," said Father Griffin. "We have to relate to the whole person, not merely to his intellect. We have to be aware of his feelings, hopes, fears, and his desire for acceptance by others. And our teaching must be experienced. An old Chinese proverb seems apt to me: 'I hear and I forget; I see and I remember; I do and I understand.'

"That Chinese proverb might well be a Japanese proverb, for these are pragmatic people. They value an idea depending on how it can be tested in this life. They feel that missionaries tend to overemphasize the spiritual and eternal, making secular life unimportant. The Japanese cannot believe that this world is unimportant."

During his university studies Father Griffin decided that the findings of psychology and of group dynamics are something a missionary might use. So he developed a course in catechetics, along with Father Sean Ryle and two Japanese instructors. The course has been developed to help people come to a degree of self-knowledge and self-acceptance so that they might be better able to accept the message of Christ.

Many people, for example, come for religious instruction full of self-rejection. Father Griffin says that self-rejection has behind it an excess of pride and that self-acceptance is necessary to humility. He has learned that accepting self is not something done once-and-for-all, but is a continuous unfolding. It is possible to accept yourself in midlife but not in old age, in health but not in sickness, in good times but not in bad.

In the new course, the first stage tries to get people to experience their own value and to see that others really do appreciate them. This stage, called pre-evangelization, consists of seventeen weekly two-hour sessions. During the first hour of each session there are group discussions and during the second hour the instructor gives a talk. The course is for small groups, eight or ten. Members are divided into even smaller groups to talk about such things as the art of listening, self-hatred, and maturity. These help people explore their feelings, to look at their self-images and to see themselves in a better light.

"At first most participants are shy and reluctant to talk," said Father Griffin, "but as the braver ones start the ball rolling, the members gradually develop a feeling of trust in one another. Others begin to speak up and tell things about themselves that they had never been able to tell anyone before. They say that they experience a feeling of great relief after unburdening themselves. Listening to shared problems makes them realize that they are not alone. This is comforting."

The second stage of the course, another four months of weekly sessions, is called evangelization. This has as its theme Encounter with Christ.

"Now we introduce the inquirer to the person of Jesus." said Father Griffin. "We try to show from Scripture what an attractive personality he is. We try to prepare the hearts and minds for the message that follows. At the end of this stage the inquirers are inducted as catechumens; this normally takes place during Sunday Mass."

The third stage, a final four months of weekly sessions, is called catechesis. The catechumen is instructed in the Christian life, the liturgy, and prayer. "The teaching of the Church is given," Father Griffin said, "but always in a way that is Christ-centered and based on the Scriptures. A textbook, a catechism which our team produced, is used for the first time. Under the old system the catechism was taught from the beginning, without any previous preparation of the inquirer's heart and mind."

Changes brought about in the lives of some of the participants have been remarkable. Changes that surprise themselves, their families, teachers, and friends. An outstanding example, Mrs. Yamashita, seventy-seven, started the course depressed and down on life. She woke up each morning hoping it would be her last so that she could join her daughter who had died. Her two married daughters dreaded visiting her; she seemed to have no time for them and was fussy and demanding.

Mrs. Yamashita found the course unpleasant at first and after each session promised herself that she would not come again. But she did. In the beginning she was a pest. She would say that her eyes were bad and that she couldn't see the blackboard, but as time went on she mellowed, and even her eyesight seemed to improve. She changed so much that people began to like associating with her and she became the group matriarch. Her teacher, Miss Yoshida, said, "You have changed from a crab apple to an apricot."

Mrs. Yamashita said that her family likes to visit her again, now that she has found new meaning in life. Instead of thinking about how much she would like to die, she wonders what she might do to help other people. She has become a counselor for other old people who come to her with troubles. She used to disdain the meetings of the elderly, but now attends them and her very presence brightens the day.

"She tells me she is busy every day," said Father Griffin. "I am impressed by her obvious deep faith."

Father Griffin does not want to give the impression that he has started a revolutionary approach to catechetics. "There is nothing really extraordinary about this course." he said. "Still the gratifying results indicate it is meeting a felt need. It is a more dynamic approach than the old method and that is one reason why all kinds of people find it appealing."

"This is just one attempt to present the Gospel message in a way that relates to the whole person. Having experienced acceptance on the human level, the inquirer is prepared to experience it on the divine level—believe that Christ accepts him or her unconditionally. This, in short, is the Good News."

Father Griffin is stationed in Fujisawa but happens to be in Tokyo just now to conduct a workshop. It is a three-day workshop for priests, sisters, and laymen, sixty-six in all, who want to learn the new system.

Columbans have done volunteer work at the Tokyo English Life Line, known as TELL. The free telephone counseling service is sponsored by English-speaking churches: the Toyko Baptist Church, the Franciscan Catholic Chapel Center, the Toyko Union Church, St. Paul's Lutheran Church, and St. Alban's Episcopal Church.

Missionaries form the backbone of the telephone service, acting as supervisors of the volunteer workers. Fathers Griffin, Sean Ryle, and Michael Healy have worked as supervisors.

Problems that come over the phone can be filed under many headings—suicide, religion, sex, marriage, pregnancy, hate, greed, and on and on.

Perhaps more calls could be filed under the heading of loneliness than anywhere else. Father Griffin recalls the night an American woman staying in a hotel in Tokyo asked the way to a certain department store. It turned out that the information was not very important to her; she really wanted the chance to talk to somebody about her loneliness.

"Indeed, loneliness and frustration are the two most common hazards foreigners face here in Tokyo," Father Griffin said. "Thrown into a strange culture, baffled by a language barrier, they feel lost and insecure."

While the missionaries do other work when not taking their turns on TELL, Father Griffin thinks that such telephone counseling is important. "This is carrying out the Christian service of *listening*. For me, listening is a high form of love.

"Here in Japan, which suffers from the problems of all industrialized countries, alienation and depersonalization cause people to struggle with burdens they can share with no one. Many have no one to listen to them. Many are afraid to talk face-to-face about their problems and prefer, until trust is built up, to remain anonymous."

Although thirty years have passed, Father Griffin remembers how terrified he was of the Japanese language. "Older priests assured us—Job's comforters they were—that we could hope for reasonable proficiency in seven years. Others, less cruel, said four years. Yet we were to have only one year's study before going to work among the people."

The seven Columbans in Father Griffin's language class, held in the Columban house in Toyko, felt blessed with an excellent Japanese teacher. He spoke English well, having lived in London for years, and so could explain in terms the young missionaries understood a difficult point of syntax or unusual turn of speech. Unfortunately they lost him to the University of Saint Louis.

Lectures were held each morning from nine until eleven and in the afternoon from two to three. The rest of the hours were spent in study. Saturday and Sunday were free.

The author of their textbook advised students to speak Japanese on every occasion: to servants, taxi-drivers, and shop assistants, and to continue to speak it "even when the other person answers you in quite good English." The author warned, "Don't go about giving free lessons in English."

With that admonition in mind the young priests went about practicing their Japanese. They began on the house servants, inescapably within reach, but not completely defenseless for they had recourse to bouts of shattering laughter which hurt their pride though it did not break their spirit.

Next came the shop assistants. "*Ikura?*" "How much?" drew a rapid reply full of numerals which the students thought they had learned but had not. "Was it four *yen*, or did he say forty?" Too embarrassed to ask they held out a palm of money and let the shopkeeper make the change.

As the weeks went by, the young priests grew more confident. Verbs began to look after their tenses and nouns and adjectives became more selective in the company they kept. The students knew they were not exactly the tutor's delight but they were causing him fewer heartaches.

A former student of mine called long distance several months ago to urge me to visit Brother Zeno when in Japan. Today I learned that I am a year too late. Brother Zeno died on April 24, 1982.

When the Pope visited him in February 1981, a newspaper guessed Zeno's age as eighty-three, another as eighty-seven. When he died a year later the estimate jumped to ninety. Once when asked how old he was he said, "I, age, don't know." That was because he had been born in Poland during hectic times; few records survive the invasions of Prussian, German, and Russian armies.

Zeno and Cardinal Karol Wojtyla first met in Rome in 1971, and by the time Karol became John Paul his fellow Pole was feeling the weight of accumulated years. The Pope, however, found his friend still humorous, charming and gentle, still a familiar figure with white, flowing beard, battered hat, worn-out shoes, and much-patched leather satchel.

"Brother Zeno had a great impact on many Japanese," said Sister Reiko Yoshida, who helps Father Griffin with workshops in catechetics. "That is remarkable since today's Japan seems to have little time for religion and scant interest in Christianity. Japan is riding high on a wave of economic growth. It prides itself on its gross national product. Yet people were aware of Brother Zeno's life even though it was a challenge to the materialistic values which rule their own lives."

That such a simple man could influence sophisticated people impressed Sister Reiko Yoshida. She began writing about him. Father Griffin translated her work into English.

Zeno Zebrowski was a member of the Order of Friars Minor Conventual. He was born on a farm in Poland and worked as a farmer, tailor, cobbler, miner, ironworker, and served in the army before entering the Conventuals in 1924.

He came to Japan in 1930, with Maximilian Kolbe, of the same religious Order, to work in Nagasaki. There he helped print the first issue of a periodical, *Seibo no kishi*, that Father Kolbe started.

"He never really learned to manage the Japanese language," said Sister Reiko Yoshida. "People who knew him well still recall his expressions clothed in funny and unfamiliar syntax. There were sometimes no

111

verbs, or prepositions were missing, or his sentences were just nouns juxtaposed.

One of his sayings about himself became the title of a book written by a friend of his: 'Zeno, no time to die!' meaning he was too busy to think of dying at the time. Someone has suggested publishing a 'Zeno's Little Red Book' with his brief but pungent sayings in funny Japanese which people remember.''

Zeno amused reporters with something he said when the government decorated him for his work in social service. Asked how he felt about such an honor he pointed to the medal on his chest, "This, not need in Heaven."

The government first took notice of Zeno right after the war. Cities were in ruins and Japanese civilians and soldiers were returning from Korea, Manchuria, Taiwan, and China. People sought shelter in stations and in underground passages and built shacks under railroad bridges . Food and clothing were scarce. Where to turn!

Wherever the eyes of despair looked, they saw Brother Zeno dressed in his black soutane with a rosary around his waist and carrying his familiar black bag. He collected goods from various quarters, including the GIs, and distributed them to the needy.

"He had the ability to put new life into people who had lost hope," said Sister Reiko. "He showed them how to help themselves, how to put up with shacks and renovate old sheds, how to make them livable. He restored self-respect and the will to live."

Zeno became involved in a ragpickers' village in Tokyo called *"Ari-no-Machi"* (Ant Town). He asked a young woman, Satoko Kitahara, to look after the children. She became known as Mary of Ant Town and is still revered, long after her death, as a holy person.

When conditions bettered, Zeno found new outlets for his caring. Wherever disaster struck—earthquakes, typhoons, fires—he was on the spot bringing relief and comfort.

The day he died the story of his life was on radio and television and in newspapers all over Japan. His photo appeared in many places. Soon magazine articles and books told of his good life.

He would have been uneasy at the splendid funeral in Akabane church, in Tokyo, which his order cares for. Countless non-Christian Japanese asked to be allowed to hold a general funeral service in a public building in Tokyo to say goodbye to the man with the remarkable eyes.

A schoolgirl said in a poem:

We do not know God,
but the gentleness of the eyes
of him who knows God
sinks deep into
our hearts.

What did Brother Zeno learn about life from having lived it? Two of his quotes hold the answer:

"Human beings, I say, all same."

"It's the heart, not words" (that really matters).

May 5
Thursday

After catching our breath for a day, Father Flinn and I took the train from Tokyo to Chiba City.

A claw-like stretch of land, the Chiba peninsula extends southeast from the capital to separate Tokyo Bay from the Pacific Ocean. On the fertile soil of this prefecture Japanese troops trained just before the Second World War, in the days when the peninsula was closed to civilians and missionaries alike.

Archbishop Peter Doi of Tokyo invited the Columbans to accept responsibility for the prefecture in 1950. In the thirty-three years since, they have established ten parishes on Chiba peninsula and staffed an existing parish on Oshima island, just off the southeast coast.

At the entrance to Saint Columban church in Chiba City, is a bronze plaque of the patron saint. Next to it is a brass plate, dated November 11, 1982, commemorating the twenty-fifth anniversary of the founding of the church. The brass plate will remind future generations of what the Columban Fathers have accomplished here, said the parishioners, realizing that the missionaries will probably do what missionaries often do, turn over a well-established church to the local clergy and move on to pioneer somewhere else.

The present pastor, Father Dennis Curran, is pleased that the parishioners ordered the brass plate on their own initiative. "When I came here in 1975 I had to make ninety percent of the suggestions at the parish council meetings. Now that has been reversed. Laymen are taking the work of the church more seriously.

"Parents are becoming more concerned about their children's religious

114

education. This is refreshing because all of society works against this. On Sundays, for instance, there are youth activities that take the children's attention away from religious education.

"I have always felt that when the Japanese get enough of material things they will say that enough is enough and will seek things for the the spirit. Even now there is a growing awareness of needs beyond the material.

"They are a generous people and readily support worthy causes. In this parish they are helping a nun in her work in the Philippines. And when a worker for a civil rights movement was killed in the Philippines the people of this parish took it upon themselves to finance the education of his children.

"While the Japanese may be materialists they are not selfish materialists. I never appeal for money. Theirs is a generous response to any need."

When I admired the stained glass window in Saint Columban's church, Father Curran said that it had been designed by a former actor who had majored in nautical engineering in the university.

"It amazes you the number of people who have degrees in a certain field but work at completely different jobs."

The pastor went on to speak of some of his parishioners with pride.

"Dr. Nakajima, in his eighties, is still going strong. He treats scores of sick children every day. He loves children and works marvels with them. Long ago he began studying European literature in university and through it became interested in Christianity. This changed the course of his life; he became a doctor feeling he could live a more helpful life that way.

"Mr. Kashiwazaki was a similar case. He was working as an engineer but after becoming a Catholic decided that as a teacher he could be more effective. The fact that students call on him for help even throughout the holidays attests to his effectiveness. The wives of both of these men are equally outstanding.

"The Muratas are another unusual couple. The wife is the daughter of a Buddhist monk. The husband, a professional actor in classical Japanese drama, changed careers to become a designer of cameras and projectors for a large company. Later he became a computer expert and now has three businesses of his own.

"Yes, it is amazing the variety of things the Japanese seem to be able to do."

Father Curran spoke of rapid changes as we stood in front of the church which sits on a bluff above Chiba City with its 770,000 people. The view immediately before us scarcely existed when the church was dedicated twenty-five years ago—a clutter of smokestacks, storage tanks and long gray factory buildings, all occupy land reclaimed from the sea.

The changes startled Father Curran when he returned to Japan in 1975, having been away for seven years teaching at a seminary in Australia.

The changes continue, especially in the cost of things. "A haircut now costs four times the price it did four years ago. And with the increase of the value of the *yen* relatively, this comes to a tenfold increase. So the barber seldom sees me."

The pastor of Saint Columban's said that Chiba City has increased in population sevenfold in the past thirty years. Now it increases at the rate of ten thousand a year. People seem busier each year and constantly on the move.

"In many ways the workers are being dispensed with as their routine services are taken over by the machine," said Father Curran. "So in a one-man bus you work out your own fare, and feed it into a machine under the watchful eye of the driver. Machines also dispense tickets for trains and subways—and give you the proper change without a word. The same goes for magazines, batteries, milk, coffee, soft drinks, beer, and different kinds of food."

Another thing Father Curran noticed after a seven-year absence is that the people had changed, too. They are more affluent and more taken up with things, and less visible around the church.

"People I meet, especially after Mass on Sunday, are very pleasant—but I have come to realize that it may be weeks before I see some of them again, while others take their turn at Sunday Mass.

"Last Sunday I talked to one of our Catholics, a psychiatrist. Working as he does until nine at night, I would expect him to be able to take it easy for at least Saturday and Sunday. But no. Instead of two days off each week he is now taking one off every two weeks.

"On Tuesday night I met another of our parishioners on his way home from work at nine. He intended to read up further on his work until midnight. At this extra-busy time he does not even have Sundays off. But he does stop at 5:30 on Saturday!

"A high school girl who has just been accepted in the university of her choice came to me a few days ago. For some time she has been attracted to Christianity, but only now does she feel free enough to come and ask for instruction.

"I have met those who have come to the church searching for a short period to help them through a particular crisis. There are others who continue but irregularly. Among the latter are some who have been reading the Bible, and those who had contact with Catholic school or Sunday school. And university students, especially those doing social studies. And housewives looking for something deeper in life. And women who have been taking classes in English at the church and now want to talk about God and Faith. I remember the old couple whose son had been a Catholic for years and whose grandchildren taught them the Our Father."

Father Curran sometimes wonders if he is getting anywhere and at other times thinks that he just might be. He wishes that life started a little later in the day when he sets off at six o'clock each morning to say Mass in a convent five miles away, and yet it is that trip that often gives him most hope.

"In the sisters' kindergarten some 250 children and their parents are surely being influenced every year. But they are influenced in ways not covered by statistics. We have planted the seed and as yet the results are not obvious. But as Saint Paul wrote: 'Neither the planter nor the waterer matters—it is only God who makes things grow.'"

Up in the northern part of Chiba prefecture, in Choshi City where Father Michael O'Dwyer is pastor, the economy depends to some extent on soy sauce.

The Columban church in Choshi City is located between two soy sauce factories. A saucy smell enlivens the air of the mission compound and trucks loaded high with bottles, barrels, and tanks of the shiny black soy sauce rumble by shaking the rectory all day long.

The two factories produce thirty million gallons of sauce each year; no telling how much the dozen other factories in town produce. If placed end to end the bottles filled with sauce would reach in a year from Japan to Australia and back.

A Columban asked one of his parishioners, Anzai San, why the Japanese use so much *shoyu*, after all it is just a flavoring, not a drink. Anzai explained that the Japanese use it at almost every meal; they boil things in whole saucepanfuls; they make soup with it; they dip things in bowls of it and sprinkle it on nearly everything.

Since *shoyu* is six times as salty as sea water—although you don't notice it because it is sweet—it has a sterilizing effect when preparing raw fish and vegetables. Its strong flavor helps make appetizing many plain-tasting Japanese foods.

Choshi City was chosen as the soy sauce capital nearly four hundred years ago because its climate is warm in winter and cool in summer; the humidity is just right; there is an abundance of good water; and in the old days the river was useful in transporting the finished product to Tokyo eighty miles away.

Down on the southern coast of Chiba, Father Patrick O'Dwyer, brother of Michael in Choshi, is pastor of the church started by Columbans at Kamogawa, a fishing village. He feels that Nature regrets being so stingy with farmland and is trying to make up for it by giving Japan an abundance of fish.

The coastal waters have fish galore. Each winter more arrive in the south-flowing current of the Sea of Okhotsk. Summer brings still more in the warm Kuroshio current flowing northward from the Indian Ocean and the waters of Malaya.

One third of the world's fishermen are Japanese. In ranging the ocean from Alaska to the South Seas they catch salmon, sardine, mackerel, pollock, skipjack, tuna, cod, hake, haddock, herring, anchovy, sea bream, yellowtails, trout, shark, cybium, flying fish, bonito, eels, mullets, smelts, prawn, cuttlefish, and squids.

The Japanese housewife could rattle off all of these names and add a few dozen more.

Fishing enterprises cover a wide range. The most impressive are the giant companies with ocean-going factory ships and their fleets of attendant trawlers. Then come the medium size operations with one boat of from 20 to 200 tons. Small, but important, are the thousands of tiny family-owned smacks which never dare venture beyond offshore waters.

The casual visitor finds it a delightful scene, a fishing village tucked away between pine-covered mountain slopes, with hanging nets, and children playing in the sun. Columbans who have worked in such villages know that this is merely a pictureque facade covering hardship and want.

Father Leo Baker, riding subways and dodging traffic in Tokyo, has nostalgic memories of Kamogawa, where Father Patrick O'Dwyer is now pastor. When the Columbans searched for a site in the fishing village, thirty years ago, the only property available for a church was a small plot of land with a Japanese house and an orange grove on it.

When Father Baker took up work in the parish the orange trees became a source of amusement. Oranges, sweet and bursting with ripeness, exercise an irresistible spell on passing schoolchildren. Since there was no front gate the children took to dropping in on the Columban a dozen times a day.

118

They never raided the trees and although a tree with magnificent oranges stood just inside the open gate no one stole so much as one orange.

The children did not even ask directly for an orange, but through ingenious roundabout ways made it clear what they had come for. It was a fascinating study in child psychology.

The missionary was in the garden when two sturdy youngsters with shaven heads and well-patched clothes came in and stood watching him work. Soon they wandered over toward the orange trees to gaze at them for some minutes.

"The oranges are coloring nicely now, aren't they?" one of them said.

"Um," responded the priest and went on digging.

A pause followed while the children planned another line of attack. They set about picking up rubbish and pulling a few weeds. For good measure they pumped a tank full of water from the well.

Father Baker decided that the tankful called for three oranges. The boys accepted them with demur and with a feigned casualness as if such a gift had been the last thought to cross their minds. To strengthen that impression they dropped the oranges and went about pulling weeds. But when the pastor looked up a few moments later boys and oranges had vanished.

Next came a group of girls, steps and stairs of all ages, from babies on their sisters' backs to children of fourteen or so. They said: "*Asobi ni kimashita.*" "We have come to play." That was to assure the priest that they had not come for ulterior motives. Soon, however, one of them asked straight out for an orange, "Not for myself, but Baby simply loves oranges, don't you, Kazue Chan?"

Her companions preferred an indirect approach: "Were some of your oranges blown down yesterday? They were? Well, shall we go and pick them up for you?" Off they went and after a half hour took all they had gathered to the housekeeper in the rectory. She, of course, could not send them away without a reward.

They must have gone home and told some of their schoolmates because soon another band arrived from the same neighborhood. Having heard that the others had collected all of the windfalls, they had to dream up a different scheme, after making it clear that they, too, had come only to play. Soon it came out: "*Ojiisan, mikan no ki ga nanbon arimasu ka?*" "Old man, how many orange trees have you?" Somewhat distracted by being called a granddad while still less than thirty, Father Baker said he was not sure of the number. So the girls volunteered to count them. And of course there was payment for this essential service.

May 6
Friday

This is the day Father Flinn must have awaited with anticipation, perhaps with some anxiety. I have been aware of its approach ever since the night we exchanged our life stories riding the bus from the airport from Tokyo.

At that first meeting he told me about spending thirty years in Japan before being assigned, five years ago, to work in Australia. Now he has returned to serve as my escort, and after our journey is over he will stay on as pastor of Togane.

Today we will see Togane. It is a town of 37,000, in the neck of Chiba peninsula, between Chiba City and the Pacific Ocean.

On the train ride from Chiba City to Togane we looked at the countryside with more than usual interest. Small towns and rice fields are recurring motifs. The pace is slower and the air more tranquil than what we found in the industrialized strip of commotion between Tokyo and Chiba City.

As we stepped from the train, the view across the street was similar to that in the opening sequence of a Western movie—long, low buildings given an even more horizontal look by lines of porches running along store fronts.

Father Timothy Greaney, waiting on the platform, suggests that we walk to the church. His car has lost the will to live, and taxi drivers of Togane do not take kindly to short hauls. Besides, the church is only a few blocks away.

After passing the stores, we entered narrow streets densely lined on each side with old houses. Everything looks old enough to indicate that these parts escaped the destruction of war.

Suddenly, there stands the church and the rectory. Both are cream-colored stucco, and both have some charm in their smallness and simplicity. The church holds only twelve pews. The rooms of the house are so small, as Japanese rooms tend to be, that you expect to see *tatami* on the floor. Downstairs is a reception room, dining room, laundry and kitchen; upstairs are two bedrooms and a sitting room.

Togane's pastor, Father Greaney, started his mission work in 1948 in China. Because of the rise of an inimical Communist government he left China and came to Japan in 1949.

The dreariness of a lost war still hung over this country. Father Greaney spoke of the rubble and of the taxis with charcoal boilers fastened in back to supply motive power. Like every Columban who knew Japan right after the war, he tells of those days with a tension in his voice that indicates the memory still haunts him.

"Tokyo was in a state of shock," Father Greaney said. "People were walking around with blank faces. They lacked good clothes. They lacked good food. Such things are missed by the Japanese more than by most people."

From Tokyo he went to Nagasaki and, of course, that was going from bad to worse. During his three years there he watched a new city rise from atomic ashes.

Father Greaney has been pastor of Togane for eight years. He has seventy-six parishioners, most of them rice farmers and shopkeepers. A few commute to offices in Tokyo, a crowded train ride of two hours each way, six days a week, for they work a half-day on Saturday. The Tokyo commuters say they have moved to Togane so that their families might "live in good air."

The town of Togane has "developed for the passing crowd," as Father Greaney puts it. Its restaurants, filling stations, and shops serve travelers from Tokyo who pass through on their way to and from the fishing towns along the eastern coast.

Father Greaney, being from County Cork, grew up with Gaelic as his first language. Now he lives in a town where he alone speaks English. "It is not a lonely life, if one enjoys reading," he said pointing to books stacked all over the place.

121

"The people here are amazed that I speak Japanese. Of course they think I am an American. They think all foreigners are American."

The pastor of Togane seems amused at the Japanese need for material things and of the strange logic they use to convince themselves that they should own something new. He told us of an ancient farmhouse, decrepit with time, where, in the darkness of one of the back rooms stands a grand piano.

"Who plays the piano?" a Columban asked the grandfather.

"Nobody," said the ancient man.

"Are you going to do something about it?"

"Yes, we'll set one of the young boys to it," was the reply.

Another family displayed with pride a set of the Encyclopedia Britannica in English, but nobody in the family knew any English. They had bought it, they explained, for a two-year-old child in the expectation that he will grow up and attend an English university.

The town planners, Father Greaney said, rejected the idea of building a swimming pool because they could not afford one of official Olympic dimensions. Without practicing in a pool of official dimensions, the city fathers decided, no child will grow up to swim in the Olympics.

The people of Togane, says its pastor, are extremely health-conscious. Ailments are the great subject of discussion. At the post office yesterday he heard an elderly woman ask another if she has had any injections lately. While drinking tea the subject often gets around to operations.

"If you want to be popular here," the pastor advised Father Flinn, "arrange to have an operation. It's a great status symbol. You will be the center of attention for three days. Die and they will speak of you for four days."

We circled back to the railroad station through a new part of town. Along the main road the restaurants string out block after block. The only English words I saw in Togane were Mobil Oil at a filling station and Robin Hood, the sign on a restaurant that contained no English on the menu.

As we waited for the train Father Greaney teased Father Flinn by reminding him that he will be arriving just in time to start preparing for the silver jubilee. (The church was built in 1958 by Father Peter O'Sullivan.) Father Flinn indicated that he would gladly let the anniversary go unheralded.

The turnover of the parish was remarkably simple. Father Flinn said that he would say Mass as the new pastor of Togane on Sunday, May 29.

"Good enough," said Father Greaney, "I'll book my flight back to Ireland for the 28th."

It was all decided in less than a minute.

(Two months after becoming pastor of Togane Father Flinn sent me a few photographs and a few words. One photograph, labeled "the people meet their pastor," shows twenty of his seventy-six parishioners, all attractive people, indeed.

Father Flinn said that he had asked a Japanese seminarian: "If you were going to Togane where there are seventy-six Catholics, no car, no housekeeper, no church committee, no money in the kitty and only eighteen people at Mass on Sundays, what would you do?"

The seminarian answered, "The first thing I would do would be to look for a good part-time job!"

"A part-time job?"

"Yes, like selling soap or something," said the seminarian and added, "Perhaps praying might help a bit."

Later Father Flinn repeated this conversation to an elderly priest in Kyoto, and asked, "Do you think that the seminarian meant that the part-time job would enable me to meet people, or give me something to do, or help me to get some money?"

"We Japanese are a practical people," said the elderly priest. "I think he meant to earn some money."

According to the letter the new pastor of Togane is doing quite a bit of writing.)

On the trip back to Tokyo when the train stopped momentarily at a country station I was surprised to see graffiti scribbled on the back wall. Japan is rarely cluttered with such. A million people can pass through a subway station and leave it remarkably unlittered. It is rare to see cigarette butts or chewing gum wrappers on the street. At a horse show the other day I noticed that after thousands of people had passed through the show grounds there was no litter.

The Japanese take good care of things. I have been looking for an automobile with a dent in it, or some rust, or in need of washing. Surely I will find one trashy car before this tour is over.

As we neared the Columban Central House in Tokyo, Father Flinn said that tomorrow he will try to get a driver's license. As he recalls, getting a license used to be quite a task and he wonders if it still is. You had to face up to a course in motor mechanics, learn the rules of the road, and take a written exam, and a driving test.

Father Flinn advises foreigners who want a license to be courteous to the examiner. "I watched a tall business man storm up to the sergeant at the license center and declare through an interpreter: 'I'm a busy man and I can't wait two days. I want to drive my car today.' From the expression on the sergeant's face I doubt whether the visitor has received his license yet."

In approaching the same sergeant Father Flinn bowed Japanese style. The sergeant smilingly told him to fill in the answers to the questionnaire in pencil.

"When I had finished, he erased all the wrong answers with fitting comments: 'You meant this 60 miles to be 50, didn't you?' or 'This is 20 miles, is it not?' Each time I bowed and apologized for my ignorance. I was driving the next day."

Visitors may wonder at the disparity between the severity of driving regulations and the free-wheeling practices on Japanese roads. As Father Flinn observed, "A day at the wheel leaves you weary, bewildered, and convinced that most of Japan's roads were planned a long time before the automobile was invented." He quoted a roadside sign: "Why do you drive so fast in such a small country?"

To renew your license after three years you must attend a lecture for an hour at a police station. There you hear frightening facts about the cause and result of road accidents.

"I lost the capacity years ago to be surprised by any maneuver that a driver might make," said Father Flinn. "If I am a pedestrian I move with deliberation and give every car the right of way; if I am mowed down I will be blamed for not 'understanding the Japanese way of the road.' If I am driving and have a crash, the presumption is that being a foreigner, I am richer than the Japanese, and that I can afford to pay for the damage."

Father Flinn said that to take a taxi is not for the chicken-hearted. The drivers are out to break the sound barrier.

"If the driver stops to search for the address the passenger should pay him and get another taxi. Experienced hands tell us that once he 'loses face' he also loses his sense of direction. It is cheaper to alight then."

May 7
Saturday

The train from Tokyo to Odawara was so crowded that we had a demonstration of how passengers are able to sleep standing up. No danger that they might slide to the floor; they are too tightly packed. The marvel is that they awaken just as the train slows for their station.

My arm, extended upward gripping the strap, began to throb when the blood ran from it, but I could not lower it in that density of human beings. Now I know why "hip pushers" are hired to shove commuters into the car far enough for the doors to close. In winter, signs ask passengers not to wear overcoats unless necessary; the added bulk lowers the pay load. It is all very intimate.

Nine young people, boys and girls of senior-high age, were on the train on their way to do some mountain climbing. They were well turned out with climbing boots, woolen stockings, knee breeches, bright sweaters, and well-balanced backpacks. The Japanese always dress the part. Whether playing tennis or golf or riding horses or motorcycles, they are smartly dressed for the sport. They doubtless study the advertisements in fashion magazines. All this now that the Japanese revel in what they call the "leisure boom."

This trip that we are taking from Tokyo to Odawara by train, many young Columbans used to take by jeep as part of their orientation. Father John Vaughan, the mission procurator, became a legend as their guide on his supply run down through Kanagawa district. Once a month he prepared for this all-day jaunt. He would tilt back his hat, check the list for the last time, and pull the tarpaulin over the loaded trailer. After the young priests had climbed into the jeep he would start from Saint Patrick's, early in the morning, and rattle through the streets of Tokyo, heading for Yokohama and for four Columban missions beyond.

In 1948 Bishop Thomas Wakida of Yokohama had sent an urgent request to Ireland asking for Columban missionaries. He wanted them to staff a large section of the important prefecture of Kanagawa, taking over some existing churches and opening new ones whenever possible. It was across this territory that Father Vaughan carried supplies, mostly groceries, and a few diverse items such as clothes for the poor as well as a Christmas crib.

Within an hour after leaving St. Patrick's in Tokyo the jeep would jolt into Yokohama, the port city. Father Vaughan always steered clear of downtown and climbed a steep hill to heights overlooking the busy harbor. Suddenly he would make a sharp turn down toward the sea, rolling to a halt outside a tree-shaded dwelling that bore the small wooden sign: St. Columban's.

The house, home of the Nakamura family, was used as a language school for newly arrived Columbans. If the Misses Nakamura, graduates of St. Maur sisters' school, had not made their home available to the missionaries, the work of the Columbans would have been set back for months because no suitable housing was in sight and no one was permitted to land in Japan unless assured of a dwelling.

Father George Bellas and some of the language students would help unload the supplies. After a quick, light breakfast and an exchange of news, Father Vaughan and his passengers climbed back into the jeep to rattle up the hill and out of Yokohama.

On the way to Kamakura, Father Vaughan told the young missionaries that the parish priest, Father John Crowe, had as a neighbor the largest Buddha in the world. Sixty feet tall! An exaggeration. The statue and other shrines date back six centuries to when Kamakura was the capital of the country. Now the town is a place of pilgrimage, said Father Vaughan, and a seaside resort where many of Tokyo's leading citizens have summer houses.

After Father Crowe and his assistant, Father Peter Niland, had thanked their visitors for the groceries, the jeep lurched southward along the bay toward Katase.

Fathers Jerome Sweeney and T.J. Griffin lived in a house in Katase that Admiral Yamamoto had given to the Church. This was the elder Yamamoto who had retired before the war, Father Vaughan explained, the Yamamoto who had been tutor and traveling companion to Emperor Hirohito when the ruler was still Crown Prince.

On to Chigasaki to deliver supplies to Father Keith Gorman. The jeep eased down a narrow lane, turned into a still narrower one, and parked near an unpainted Japanese dwelling. This one-story house, under trees in a field, was church, rectory, and instruction hall. Father Vaughan reminded his passengers to be sure to kick off their shoes before entering, for this is an all-Japanese house with *tatami* on the floors.

Next Odawara, the city with a melodious name. The end of the line. (In those days the population was 80,000 and now, thirty years later, it is 178,000.) Father Vaughan's passengers were always impressed with the setting—the mountains of Hakone and Tanzawa on east and west and the Bay of Sagami on the south.

After unloading supplies at Saint Theresa, the visitors would sit down with Fathers Arthur Friel and Thomas Kilkenny for a leisurely supper and an exchange of news. The Columbans of Odawara spoke with enthusiasm about Mayor Jiro Suzuki and his city fathers. Although non-Christian, the officials of the city were pleased to have priests and nuns among them, feeling that their presence was good for the moral climate of Odawara.

Now came the difficult part. Father Vaughan did not enjoy the three-hour drive through darkness back to Tokyo. His passengers, though, had the satisfaction of knowing that they had spent a day that would stick in their memories as long as they lived.

When we came out of the train station in Odawara, Father Flinn knew that Saint Theresa's church was within an easy walk, but he did not know the direction, and so he stopped at the police station. The sergeant, explaining that the route is complicated, drew a detailed map.

The walk starts in a sophisticated shopping center, with sidewalks shaded by attractive verandas. Sophistication comes to Odawara because of its proximity to the sea and to Mount Fuji.

Down a narrow back street we located a lovely little church built a century ago by French missionaries. The pastor, Father Patrick Scully, was expecting us.

Through the years every pastor of Odawara, starting with Father Friel in 1950—has seen more than his share of visitors. That is because this is the nearest Columban rectory to Mount Fuji. Many a young missionary, seeing Fujiyama silhouetted against the blue horizon, feels the need to climb it.

Fujiyama is the most beautiful mountain in Japan, and perhaps the most famous in the world. The symmetrical cone rises 12,953 feet above sea level. Even this late in spring, May 7, snow covers more than two-thirds of the mountain.

When the mountain-climbing visitors arrive at the rectory in Odawara they are provided with a flask of water and some bread and tea. They go by train to Gotemba and from there by bus to Subashiri, a tiny village at the foot of the sacred mountain. Here they become a part of the statistic of the thousands who climb the mountain each year. They pass ten stations, each with a rest house where the pilgrim's staff is branded. On the summit are a Shinto shrine and shelters where pilgrims arriving at night await the sunrise. Here a Shinto priest stamps the pilgrim's staff with red ink to certify that the sacred ascent has been completed.

The climb is arduous but not dangerous. For the first 1,500 feet the slopes are cultivated. From there a grassy pastureland stretches to 4,000 feet. Forest covers the next 4,000 feet. Beyond the forest stretch wide spaces of ash and broken lava. At the summit is the awe-inspiring crater.

Father Patrick Diamond climbed Fuji with four other Columbans and described the experience in some detail. He said that when they reached Subashiri they bought pilgrims' staffs and felt excited about the coming adventure.

As they began their ascent it was still warm even though the sun was setting—a ball of fire behind the mountain. Soon they were in open country with no house in sight, an unusual experience in densely populated Japan. The road narrowed to a path. Darkness fell suddenly.

After what seemed many hours of trudging—it was really only two—they came to the first station at eight o'clock. The five of them agreed that this was enough walking for the first day and decided to stop for the night. It was a tactical blunder, as they later realized. The Japanese never halt at the first station on the first night but push on to the fourth or fifth.

Having washed off the dust and removed their shoes the missionaries entered the rest house. It was built of logs and housed a Japanese family who attended to the wants of pilgrims. The new arrivals submitted their staffs for branding.

While sitting around a fire in the center of the room they cooked a meal and brewed some tea. The Japanese drink a green tea which is excellent for quenching thirst, but on this occasion the Irishmen felt that something stronger was called for and so drew on their own supplies of black tea.

"After the meal we sat on cushions around the fire and attempted to converse in Japanese," said Father Diamond. "We were on holiday from language school in Yokohama. Asked where we came from we replied 'Ireland,' to the visible consternation of our hosts who understood us to mean that we had travelled specially across the world to climb Mount Fuji. I am not sure we succeeded in correcting that impression."

The hosts unrolled beds for their guests: cotton-filled mattresses, cylindrical pillows filled with rice hulls, and cotton-padded silk-covered quilts. The beds were comfortable because they were spread on straw matting two inches thick.

The priests were awakened at 5:30 in the morning to the call of "*Okite kudasai.*" "Get up, please!" After a hurried breakfast and a bow to their hosts the five were off up the steep trail. In the cold darkness they were surprised to see looming on the trail ahead a solitary human figure with a pack mule carrying supplies to stations up the mountain.

At the second station the missionaries again had their staffs branded and replenished the water in their flasks. Upon emerging from the upper fringe of the forest belt, they looked back to see the valley far below in morning mist. As the sun climbed the mist dispersed revealing villages nestled around the mountain's base with Lake Yamanaka and the woods that fringe its shore.

"The heat came down on us," said Father Diamond. "We realized why those who climb Mount Fuji try to cover most of the ground during the cool of the evening and early night. We reached the eighth station hot, weary, and perspiring and looking beyond it at the two stages that still separated us from the summit we felt strongly tempted to turn back. But then there were our staffs, awaiting that final, official seal to say that we had conquered the sacred mountain. And as we rested and debated we were joined by an old man and his son, returning from the summit. The father had made the pilgrimage many times and was still making it at seventy-four. There could be no question of our yielding after that."

The five Columbans finally reached the top and looked down on the rich panorama below. In early and middle summer Japan is clothed with the fresh, velvety-green foliage that visitors from less temperate climates find charming. Occasional wisps of while clouds floated lazily below. Here and there in gullies on the mountainside traces of snow still lingered, glistening in the brilliant sunlight. To the east on the horizon was a glimpse of the sea.

"We feasted our eyes for some time on all this glory, before turning to take a brief look at the crater," Father Diamond recalled. "It takes an hour to walk around it, but we did not verify that because we could not delay. Now we had our staffs branded for the last time: "Sunrise Top, Mount Fuji, 12,953 feet."

By late evening the five bone-tired missionaries were back in Odawara enjoying the genial hospitality of a Columban rectory.

Father Vincent Youngkamp—we met him ten days ago in Kumamoto—made the mistake of talking to a tall lean American paratrooper about climbing Mount Fuji.

"Really, Father, it's nothing but a long walk up a hill," said the soldier. "Of course, I'm in fairly good condition. I jump once a month, and exercise about three hours every morning. Oh, yes, not everybody made the summit. I'd say about forty percent. It was biting cold the night I climbed. The rain was icy."

When Father Youngkamp and another Columban decided to climb Fuji they took a bus marked Fifth Station. Since there are ten stages in the Fuji climb, if this bus took them to number five it should be a breeze from then on.

The only vehicles the bus met on the way up were other buses and lumber trucks. Meeting them on a narrow road meant backing to a clearing to let them pass. It meant also, on each occasion, a heated exchange between the drivers.

As the bus climbed the air grew steadily crisper. Darkness fell. One by one the lights went on across the mountain.

At the fifth station somebody tugged at the Columbans' knapsacks and said, "Me, guide, 2,900 yen." The American paratrooper had said that a guide is unnecessary, and so the missionaries decided to save the nine dollar fee. The guide shrugged his shoulders and muttered, "fool," and walked away. No one volunteered to offer directions.

The two priests started up a road and met three Western teenagers whose eyes were bloodshot, faces sunburned and clothes dirty. They had set out in the afternoon sun. The boy said, "I made the top, these girls didn't. It's awful." He seemed tired and confused.

In parting the Columbans wished the teenagers good luck. The boy quipped, "You'll need it more than we do."

From the fifth to the seventh stage was easy enough. The path provided sure, firm footing. A little steep, perhaps, but simple enough, especially after the moon came up.

Along the way the two Columbans took in tow an American travel agent who felt the incline at every breath. Fifty years old and two hundred pounds in weight, he was in trouble. By the seventh station he needed to rest. At 12:30 A.M. the three adventurers stopped at a *hoteru*.

Although called a hotel it was only a straw-matted hut, with a floor crowded with sleepy-eyed climbers rolled in blankets.

"Have you a quieter place?"

The *hoteru*-keeper brought out a ladder.

The rafters, too, were crowded. And so the three settled on the floor. After some minutes of restless sleep the Columbans rose at 2:30 A.M., but the tourist agent slept on.

Only an hour and a half to reach the top for the sunrise! There was a sense of urgency among the climbers who passed the priests at half trot. The going was harder, the gradient steeper and the air thinner. By the eighth station the Columbans needed more frequent pauses for breath. By the ninth they felt like giving up.

Father Youngkamp said, "We'll walk for five minutes and rest for two. I'll keep time." Even with that plan there was a pressure in the chest and some nausea.

At four o'clock sharp they reached the top, just as the sky was lightening. The sun came up, as a rim of red and grew into a glowing, burning circle, lighting the land and lakes and ocean far below. From that moment on the two Columbans always agreed with people who say that the best view of Japan is from the top of Mount Fuji.

Nine hours to climb; six to descend. Father Youngkamp suggested that they go down by way of Gotemba, just because it is a different route, not knowing about the volcanic ash. The missionaries struggled through the drifts of it, sinking a foot at every step. It was torture, especially in tennis shoes.

Upon reaching the bottom at 9:30 A.M. they shook the volcanic ash from their shoes for the last time. Then for a meal of rice and lamb strips, one fit for Fuji climbers!

A veteran of the climb has a few tips: "Make sure you are trim, under thirty years of age, and weigh under 170 pounds. Wear a high, comfortable pair of boots. Bring a sweater and a raincoat, just in case. Choose a clear moonlight night in July or August. Set aside two days for the climb, and another two days to unbend and ease some of those aches. Bring a flash-light and some rations. Have a sportman's wish to hit the top."

With all of this in mind Father Flinn and I are not tempted to challenge Fuji.

The three of us—Father Patrick Scully, Father Kevin Flinn, and I—sat in the rectory of St. Theresa's church in Odawara and talked late into this Saturday night. Most of the talk had to do with the character of the Japanese, and the problem of serving these admirable people.

It is good to see the affection Father Scully has for his parishioners. He admires their "strong spiritual base," but admits that "something is driving them on the materialistic side."

The demands made by materialism may be getting too abrasive, he said, and told an anecdote about a rebel he met lately.

"A man near here works in a bank. He is well up toward the top and it is a big bank. The other night he came here to the house at ten o'clock. He was on his way home but stopped here first because he did not want to take his troubles to his wife. He said he rarely gets home before eleven at night. He even works on Saturday and brings home a stack of work and is often at it until dawn. He sees his children only when they are asleep. 'I am fed up to the teeth,' he told me. 'But what can I do! I have a family to support.' It is evident he is at the end of his tether."

Father Scully recalled, "The people came through a period of having nothing. They worked like slaves to get back on their feet. It was a heady experience and they were happy in their materialistic prosperity.

"A dozen years ago the first signs of disillusionment began to show. University students saw that this kind of prosperity can be dehumanizing. They said so.

"The older people didn't agree at the time. They still remembered how bad things used to be. But now people of all ages are beginning to realize that there is more to life than material prosperity."

Father Flinn agreed that the youth of Japan are becoming dissatisfied with the old intensities. He said that a government survey reports: "Man is unhappy because he must work mechanically, like a cog in a machine, and not in a human fashion. Too much emphasis on industrial development tends to make people unhappy."

Both priests agreed that dissatisfaction begins at home. "The young Japanese feels," observed Father Flinn, "that his home life is not what it should be. For one thing, he thinks that his mother should broaden her view of life. And in school the students complain that teachers communicate information mechanically and place too much emphasis on memorizing, when they ought to be teaching with more creativity."

I said that listening to them talk about how there is a general relaxing of the old ways makes me recall something I heard about the change in the Jap-

132

anese formal bow. The angle of the bow is contracting. Maybe that is an outward sign of an inward feeling. The bow of youth used to be almost ninety degrees. Young people now do not bow nearly so low as their fathers did.

I asked Father Scully if there will be a growth in Christianity in Japan in the near future.

"There won't be any mass conversions," he said, "but there are an awful lot of people thinking."

He went on to explain that there is a different approach to mission work. "Ten or fifteen years ago I thought you had to baptize them to be successful. We counted numbers and kept lists. Now that I know more about the love of God, I know that if we don't baptize them they may be saved anyway. Now missionaries concentrate on the good points in the Japanese people. There is so much we can learn from them."

Father Scully seems to agree with something I have heard other missionaries say: The greatest contribution a missionary can make in Japan is not to preach a certain dogma but to live the kind of life that Japanese might admire and imitate. To oversimplify, he needs to present a kind of balance between the ascetic and the aesthetic.

Yesterday Father Scully received a letter from a contractor saying that for the next few months he would be doing some building in the neighborhood of Saint Theresa's church and so would be making something of a pest of himself. He apologizes for whatever inconvenience he might cause, and please accept this gift.

The gift was the most handsome bath towel I have ever seen.

On another occasion a contractor sent a lovely *furoshiki* which Father Scully gave me to take home to my wife.

A *furoshiki* is a simple piece of cloth ranging in size from one foot square to twelve times that. What would the Japanese do without it! Its versatility amazes me. Sometimes it serves as an umbrella for a lady caught in a shower, or a substitute for a missing radiator cap, or a sling for a broken arm. It has swallowed such astonishing bulks as a child's tricycle, rolls of bedding, and a piece of furniture.

I'm told that the *furoshiki* was first used in the fourteenth century in a palace in Kyoto. So as not to get clothing wet from water tracked from bathroom to dressing room the courtiers began wrapping their clothes in a large cloth and the cloth got the name of *furoshiki*, "bathroom spread."

The contractor who sent Father Scully a gift was not a rare soul; this happens often. I heard of a contractor who gave new linoleum for a church's parish hall and a widow a new fence, all by way of apology for the noise and commotion his builders would cause in the neighborhood.

Father Flinn said that what the contractor did is a reflection of the Japanese custom of persistent gift giving. For example, one gift season is *O-chugen*, from mid-June to mid-July; another is *O-seibo*, during December, and another, *O-nenga*, in January.

"Among young people, especially, gifts are exchanged at Christmas and on birthdays," he said, "but the gift bombardment goes on even when there is no special occasion. A Japanese would never think of returning home from a trip, for instance, without bringing an *o-maige*, a present for the folks at home, which includes relatives, friends, and workers at the office.

"Gifts are expected when a person is sick, or when some relative dies. They are expected when one suffers from an accident, fire, flood, or sets out on a journey. Or when someone does you a service."

To ensure that obligations are fulfilled, a strict record of all gifts received must be kept, especially on the occasion of a funeral or when one goes to the hospital. Later on when the person who gave the gift has a funeral in the family or becomes sick the exact same amount must be returned.

The Japanese have some sayings: "If you wish to receive, first give." "Giving is for the purpose of receiving." "Give with the hope of a bigger return."

When Father Arthur Friel was appointed pastor here in Odawara in 1950, he became a part of the remarkable life story of the aging Shuichi Asano. Early in life Mr. Asano had become a millionaire and the owner of the Fuji Film Company, which in the world of Japanese photography was as important as being head of Eastman Kodak.

Father Friel instantly recognized that Mr. Asano was a great gentleman: "He was cultured and literary," observed the Columban, "and combined in his manner the magnificence of a grandee of old Spain and the imperturbability of the true Confucian scholar."

Although he had no son—and as an Oriental he felt that as a lack in his life—he did have a daughter, Aiko. He had so much pride and delight invested in her that when she became a Catholic in 1938 she made every effort to keep the matter secret from her father. When she eventually admitted what she had done, he showed his displeasure.

Aiko undermined every plan her father had for her to get married; she wanted to go to the convent. She told her pastor that she hoped to join the

Trappistines, and to her surprise the old French missionary told her that her place was with her father.

During the Second World War, Mr. Asano developed tuberculosis and Aiko was glad that she had stayed at home for now she could nurse him past the crisis. For seven years Mr. Asano watched Christianity in action in the daily life of his daughter. Slowly he came to the conclusion that she had found what he had longed for all of his life—a faith in something beyond the material.

One day in the autumn of 1945, Shuichi Asano called Aiko to his room and told her he wanted her to enter the convent of the Trappistines. He was about to become a Catholic, he said.

After several months of instruction, he was baptized as Francis Xavier by Father Hino, the Japanese priest who was pastor of Odawara between the time the French missionaries left and the Columbans arrived. Toward the end of 1945 Aiko entered the convent.

When Father Friel became pastor of Odawara the first person to whom he administered Extreme Unction was Shuichi Asano. The two men became close friends and as the end drew near the Japanese asked the missionary to come twice a day to pray with him. Whenever the priest arrived he found the old man's fingers slipping over a worn pair of rosary beads.

Mr. Asano's funeral was the biggest in the memory of anyone in Odawara. His friends and associates crowded in from all over Japan. Every member of the Catholic community was there. Nine Columbans came from their parishes in the Yokohama district to pay their respects.

As the small urn containing the remains was placed on a stand by the vault before being committed to the tomb, Father Friel fulfilled Shuichi Asano's last wish. The Columban removed the lid of the urn and dropped on the grey, charred bones the worn rosary.

May 8
Sunday

The train trip from Odawara to Fujisawa takes about forty minutes along the coastline of Sagami Bay. In that time we passed near Columban churches at Kozu, Ninomiya, Oiso, Hiratsuka, Chigasaki, and Katase.

A missionary referred to the church in Fujisawa, with its 2,500 parishioners, as "the flagship of the Columbans in Japan." Upon stepping into the compound I knew what he meant. It was alive with people greeting each other on the way to the 9:30 Mass. The buildings enclosing the compound are well designed and well kept. The large octagonal church, with walls of opaque glass, is Oriental in feeling and not a European import.

This Mass was overflowing, although there are four others today. The celebrant was the pastor, Father Cathal Gallagher, thirty-three, who speaks with an accent as thick as the tweed made in his native Donegal. During the sermon I wondered how a Donegal accent sounds to the Japanese. Surely it is there, because priests said that they used to be amused when a Japanese boy at the language school imitated their Kerry, Cork, and Dublin accents trying to come to terms with the Japanese tongue.

Father Gallagher organized his parishioners to give a helping hand to the Vietnamese boat-people living in Fujisawa. It started when Japanese cargo ships rescued refugees from overcrowded, leaky boats.

The Japanese government did not greet the refugees with open arms, but various organizations tried to make them feel welcome. Soon housewives, university students, priests, and nuns were out on the street begging. They

136

collected about $5,000 and great quantities of clothes, blankets, furniture, and kitchenware.

Father Gallagher aimed at bigger things. He decided to raise $20,000 to renovate a decaying building that refugees were using. Seeing this, the Rotarians offered to pay for kitchens and bathrooms. Parishioners and refugees made items that could be sold at bazaars. Soon the money was there.

The government, perhaps embarrassed by the efforts of individuals, built a resettlement center that would house 150 refugees. University students volunteered to go to the center to teach the kinds of skills needed to get a job. They also visited factories and businesses asking that refugees be employed. Each month it is easier for them to find jobs because the Vietnamese enjoy a good reputation as diligent, honest, reliable workmen.

A Columban observed: "To visit the Vietnamese, especially in the evening when most of them are at home, is a heart-warming experience. The first thing you realize is that these are not nameless, faceless groups the like of which the words 'boatpeople' or 'refugees' conjure up. They are a community of very human, lovely, and lovable people. The children especially steal your heart now that they are beautiful, happy, and healthy. What a contrast to those emaciated bodies with the sad, sad faces, old beyond their years, who landed in Japan. It is inspirational to see how the Vietnamese live in harmony and help one another.

The Columbans agree that the refugees did as much for the parish of Fujisawa as the parish did for them. They helped unite the parishioners in the spirit of generosity and mutual help. One Columban said, "Everyone is glad that the Vietnamese came to this area."

Each missionary has a collection of anecdotes about characters he has come to know. Priests here in the parish of Fujisawa—Fathers Cathal Gallagher, Patrich Bradley, and Gerald Griffin—can tell anecdotes galore about Kanai San.

When that vagrant began hanging around the church compound, Father Gallagher gave him small jobs to do, such as sweeping up and collecting rubbish. In this way Kanai San earned a little money.

It is a case of here today and gone tomorrow, for Kanai San has an itch to travel. In his specialty of visiting churches all over Japan he is ecumenical; he gladly seeks help from all denominations. Upon returning to Fujisawa he tells stories about how so-and-so San in such-and-such a place gave Kanai San some work to do around the church and how the "teacher" in another church was good and helpful. It is almost as though he is reporting on a contest to see who can do the most for Kanai San.

Father Griffin asked him how he was able to travel so much with so little income. The nomad said he always buys the minimun fare ticket. Once on the train it is a contest to see if he can evade the conductor for a couple of hundred miles. He has come to think of it as his right to ride the train for minimum fare. When told that the National Railways were increasing the minimum from 80 yen to 120 yen he became angry and denounced such lack of responsibility. But the new minimum did not deter his travels.

Through the years Father Griffin has pieced together Kanai San's life story. He came from the north Kyushu in western Japan, and was inducted into the army but was not sent overseas. His buddies never reached their destination; they were all drowned when a torpedo hit their ship. Upon returning home after the war he found that his parents and most relatives were dead; his only brother had died in New Guinea.

As a day laborer he gradually worked his way to Tokyo. Since Kanai San is rather simple, people took advantage of him along the way. He has a long history of being fooled by the unscrupulous and of having his money taken from him. After getting to Tokyo he managed to get a shoeshine kit and was able to make a bit of money. Gangsters tried to make him pay for protection and when he refused to pay, the hoodlums drove him out of business.

Kanai San told Father Griffin that twice he has considered suicide. Once, when he had tuberculosis he was so sore from getting injections that he wrote a suicide note, but when he tried to choke himself it was so painful he gave up.

Another time he decided to throw himself under a train. A policeman saw him standing around and arrested him for loitering. In the jail the policeman gave a bowl of hot noodles to the vagrant who had not eaten anything so delicious in a long time.

Later when Kanai San got a job as a day laborer he used his first pay to buy a box of cookies and took them to the policeman. Touched by the gesture, the policeman said it was the first time he ever received anything from anyone he had helped.

When one of the Vietnamese refugees died, Kanai San sat all night in front of the coffin in Fujisawa church. He played his harmonica in semi-darkness to console the dead man's spirit.

"He seems never to have established his own identity," said Father Griffin. "He always refers to his name, Kanai, when talking about himself, instead of using the word 'I.' It is as if he were speaking about someone else.

"This may be because he had received so little kindness in his lifetime, met with so little respect, and kicked about by everyone, treated as a nonentity, nonperson, in a society that has no place for people like him."

Father Gallagher was able to get Kanai San a small hut to live in at the back of the church yard. The city paid for it. With a fixed abode the former vagrant is now eligible for social welfare and benefits.

The priests tease him about being a "capitalist." They call him the president of Kanai's Trust Bank. He enjoys the banter. His weakness now is playing the *pachinko* machines, a kind of slot machine. He can spend a whole day in front of them without tiring. He claims he comes away a winner every time.

A couple of Christmas Eves ago, the church in Fujisawa was packed. After the Gospel, a line of twenty men and women stood in front of the altar to be baptized. After the ceremony they were introduced as new members of the Christian community. As each rose there was warm applause. The ovation was thunderous when shy, frail Kanai San stood up.

Some striking flower arrangements, left from yesterday's wedding, enhance the church in Fujisawa today. The bride and groom happened to be members of the parish, but they might as well have been non-Christians for thousands of such get married in Catholic churches each year.

The Japanese state recognizes no religious ceremony and has no wedding rite of its own. As far as the state is concerned just a little paperwork is necessary to register a marriage.

Many young people want a church wedding because they attended Catholic schools. Some see marriage as a turning point in their lives and wish to mark it in a special way.

After attending a church wedding, a Japanese gentleman said to a Columban: "I really felt those young people were doing something important. The only thing I remember of my marriage is three days of drinking *sake*. Could my children, even though not Christian, get married like that?"

The prospective bride and groom bring their family registers to the rectory to prove that they have not been married. The priest deposits copies in the church archives. The couple must also attend a premarital course.

Father Noel Doyle used to give a talk at the wedding about marriage as a lasting vocation. About half the brides would cry. "One day the bride started crying during my talk," said Father Doyle. "Some of the guests joined in. At the marriage promise, the bridegroom was crying so hard it was difficult to get a response from him. I decided it was time to change my talk."

The state of matrimony in Japan is something else Father Flinn has written about. He finds that the matchmaker is returning to power because marriages for love and those arranged by computers have been unsatisfactory in this culture.

Father Flinn quotes a go-between who is to matchmakers what Babe Ruth is to ballplayers. The seventy-five-year-old, named Cupid of the Year, boasts that there were only five divorces out of the 3,100 marriages he helped arrange. He hopes to live until ninety so that he will have time to bring together 10,000 couples.

Cupid of the Year waxed eloquent when telling his success story: "Matchmaking requires a great deal of thought as well as time. One has to be sure that the right people are brought together. Education, character, family background must be taken into consideration. I don't even think a long-faced woman should marry a long-faced man. They will have long-faced children, and even grandchildren.

"You have to be a kind of social worker, seeing to it that the timid and the handicapped are helped as much as possible. The Japanese say 'There is a lid for every pot.' To find the proper fit, that is the go-between's job.

"A good go-between also does his best to keep the couple together after marriage. When disputes arise—and it takes three disputes before a couple settles down—he acts as mediator.

"He must be a good judge of character. The busybody type of go-between will be a nuisance. The conscientious one will become more needed as life grows more complicated."

Love marriages were condemned by traditional Japanese society. They were called indiscretions, sins, blunders and, in some cases, crimes. Novels and Kabuki plays tell about the inevitable tragedy of love affairs.

Father Flinn believes that the return to arranged marriages can be traced to the great number of young people hurt and disappointed by love affairs or hasty love marriages. Two thirds of all divorces are from love marriages. The once rebellious Japanese youth realize the value of the age-old Japanese counseling system. Parents, friends, and the go-between are asked to lend assistance.

"The favorite kind of marriage, " said Father Flinn, "is the cross between the traditional arranged match and the modern love match. In this system young couples are introduced after a thorough investigation of their backgrounds, and then gradually fall in love in the course of repeated meetings. Of course they may fall in love first, then find some suitable third party to make investigations and to arrange their marriage for them."

Those investigations, according to Cupid of the Year, require the touch of a master: "The *kikiawase*, the asking about, is surreptitious but exhaustive. One checks on unpaid debts, undesirable occupations, criminal records, connections with outcast families, friends, and enemies, and zodiac signs. Then there are sicknesses presumed to be hereditary—leprosy, insanity, venereal disease, tuberculosis. On the man's side you must check weaknesses even down to color blindness."

As for computerized marriages there are five companies with five hundred branch centers. Before one can feed hopes and fears into the computer there is a matter of answering 755 detailed questions.

A common request profile by a male stipulates that an ideal bride, five years younger, ought not smoke nor wear glasses. She ought to be a senior-high or junior-college graduate.

Women hope for engineers with university degrees or for public servants. The man must make a handsome salary.

The computerized marriage, the love marriage, and the arranged marriage are all competing for position. The matchmaker is out front; more than sixty percent of the marriages in Japan this year are of his arranging.

Father Patrick Bradley, himself of retirement age, works with the elderly of Fujisawa. Since Japan is a greying society, his work becomes more important each year.

Until recently this country had an advantage over Western nations because its population was young and vigorous. Now its population is aging faster than that of the United States, Britain, West Germany, and France.

The aged are still not a burden here. In 1980 taxes and social security contributions leveled by the government were only 28 percent of the gross national product. In the United States they were 33 percent, in Britain 42 percent, in West Germany 44 percent, and France 48 percent. (All of this is according to the Organization for Economic Cooperation and Development.)

The statistics are changing. By the year 2025, when the age of the industrial societies reaches its peak, Japan Economic Planning Agency forecasts that 21 percent of Japanese will be over 65, compared with 20 percent of West Germans, 19 percent of Britains, and 16 percent of Americans.

Father Bradley thinks the Japanese are living longer because their living conditions have improved so much. In the past 25 years, the life expectancy of Japanese women has risen from 68 to 80 years, and of men from 64 to 74. (In the United States life expectancy is 78 for women and 70 for men.)

Father Flinn feels sorry for the elderly of Japan: "They are put out to grass at fifty-five with plenty of life left. They no longer have patriarchal privileges. They used to have a clearly defined place and function in life, something the human spirit needs. Now they lose 'face' in the community."

He points out that September 15, designated as Respect for the Aged Day, is the very day that many of the elderly commit suicide. More old people kill themselves in Japan than in any other place in the world. Father Flinn believes they find life unbearable because of loneliness, despair, financial worries, and illness. Many can no longer stand the noise and pollution created by jammed highways and the general pace of life. So they seek out a river, a piece of rope, a gas range, or a bottle of insecticide.

Father Bradley said he thinks it is good that the elderly are beginning to learn to live on their own. In the old system when the daughter-in-law came to live in the home of the mother-in-law the arrangement often made for a horrible life for the younger woman. In other words, Father Bradley is working too closely with the elderly to become weighted with sentimentality.

The state's 1,014 Old People's Homes are ill-equipped. To save "face" the state is looking for ways to improve the lot of those who can no longer care for themselves. The Church conducts 36 such homes for 2,079 old people, a token assistance considering that 10 percent of Japan's population is over 65.

On our way back to Tokyo we stopped in Kamakura. From my afternoon here I will remember the Great Buddha and the thousands of small statues that stand in military array around the temples.

While Father Flinn went about his business taking photographs I sat down for a good look at the Great Buddha which towers thirty-three feet in the air. The face is almost eight feet high; the eyes four feet across.

The idea for it was born in 1195 when one of the rulers of Japan saw the Great Buddha of Nara and decided that Kamakura should have one, too. First came an image in wood, destroyed by a storm within a decade. The present bronze was completed in 1252.

For more than seven centuries it has been sitting here in repose, weathering the storms of nature and the wars of men, no small achievement even for bronze. Perhaps Kamakura was also on Dr. Warner's list of places that must not be bombed.

At a temple nearby I find the thousands upon thousands of small statues, each about a foot tall, even more startling than the Great Buddha. Here they stand, all these little gods, too many to count, put here by the faithful by way of supplication.

Father Flinn wrote a magazine article about the statues of Jizo, a Buddhist saint who foregoes *nirvana* for himself so that he can help others on the way. He is the protector of infants. The faces on his statues are tender and innocent, like those of children. He is decked out in red bibs and caps and recently has been given yellow plastic raincoats, knitted shawls, and baseball caps. The Japanese have made him the patron of infants who have died of starvation, infanticide, or abortion. Mothers who feel guilty about abortion attend Mizuko Kuyo services in honor of Jizo. Afterward they leave messages at the temple: "My baby, I am sorry. You came too early for us." "I came here to apologize. I feel guilty." "Please forgive your foolish father."

All of these statues caused Father Flinn to recall the time he went to Beppu to visit the famous hot-spring resort in Kyushu. In a dimly lit, steamy passageway he eased his way through caves that featured ghostly scenes of men being tortured by demons in every imaginable way. The scenes were taken from the Book of Hell and the Book of Hungry Devils written a thousand years ago.

Such legendary monsters are called *oni*. From early childhood the Japanese are in close touch with the *oni*. A baby born with teeth is called an "*oni* baby" because *oni* are supposed to have sharp teeth. Children play the *oni* game, one similar to the game of tag. Children's books are full of *oni* with full-page illustrations showing the ferocity of the red-faced, hairy giants with horns, gaping mouths and menacing fangs, wearing tiger skins and brandishing spiked clubs.

Civil wars from A.D. 1000 to 1400 caused many people to think that the Age of Decadence foretold by the Buddha was at hand. An abundance of *oni* appeared in literature; one volume, the Book of Disease, shows *oni* lining the edges of the Road of Life to glare at human beings as they pass by.

If you ask a group of Japanese, "What is an *oni*?" the ready answer is "a demon." If you ask, "What kind of demon?" no two answers are the same.

May 9
Monday

On the wall of the sitting room of the Convent of the Good Samaritan, a poster says: "The starting points of human destiny are little things." The three of us, who combine about two hundred years of living, agree with that for it has certainly been our experience.

Father Flinn brought me to the convent to meet Sister Julian McKenna, who arrived in Japan from Australia three years after the bombing of Nagasaki. She recalls that the rubble was still deep, chimneys leaned at dangerous angles, and at times she saw workmen digging bodies out of the debris as they prepared to rebuild the city.

Here in Tokyo, Sister runs a student dormitory called Holy Peace. Sixty-six Japanese girls, all university students, live here.

"Few are Christian," said Sister Julian. "Yet their values are Christian values. I feel we should deepen those values."

Although the nun did not suggest that they do so, almost every girl is reading the Bible and attending meetings to discuss what was read. They see the Bible as a classic, one of the great books of world literature.

Father Flinn observed that this is another instance of the Bible Boom which in a recent year brought about the sale of six million copies in Japan. He spoke of a friend, a layman, who arises at 3:30 each morning to read the Bible.

"Although Bible reading is the 'in thing' it can still occasion snide remarks," Father Flinn said. "Most middle school students who have a Bible carry it wrapped in newspaper to avoid comments.

"A hippie I met in Wakayama told me he had tried everything—drugs, booze, sex—and even contemplated suicide. Another hippie put him onto the Bible, marked several passages and said, 'You're right in seeking happiness. You're looking in the wrong places. What you're looking for is in this book.' It took him a while to believe it. After a training period he began working as a missionary among the hippies of Japan."

When Sister Julian made some reference to Pope John Paul's visit to this country, I told her that wherever we have gone people have spoken of it.

In Ryujin, Father Eamonn Horgan admitted that when he heard of the proposed visit his misgivings were strong, as were those of other missionaries. Is this the proper time? Aren't there too few of us in Japan to rate a visit? Will the Japanese ignore him? Is late winter the best season? Will the media give anything but a minimum of coverage?

Father Horgan admits he was wrong on every fear. In the worst of weather enthusiastic crowds gathered. The media were never more generous. A vast audience followed, hour-after-hour, the four-day visit on "live" television.

In Chiba City, Father Dennis Curran had told us that the pontiff's visit has left a mark on the Japanese consciousness. For instance, when the Emperor was asked what was the most important thing that had happened to him in the past year he answered, "Meeting the Pope."

Father Curran told of the daughter of a Buddhist monk who upon becoming a Catholic was treated as an outcast by relatives and friends. After the Pope's visit, however, they embraced her, saying that now they realize why she did what she did.

In Togane, Father Timothy Greaney spoke of how favorably the visit had impressed the people in his town. "They were most impressed that he went to the trouble to learn Japanese. He did it, I'm told, by having a Japanese priest have breakfast with him every morning for ten weeks. Although he spoke from a prepared manuscript his accent was more than acceptable."

The young people of Togane sometimes speak to Father Greaney about the time "your man from Rome was here." On the day the Pope was shot, people Father Greaney had never seen before stopped him on the street to express sympathy.

In Odawara, Father Patrick Scully had said, "The Pope's visit changed the outlook of Japanese society as to what the Catholic Church stands for. Changed it to a remarkable degree. We used to be almost a whipping post, but no more. I doubt that any Catholic country gave the Pope's visit such positive coverage and so much of it.

"Mother Teresa also has been a great influence in Japan. People come up to me to tell me how much they admire those two. Yes, the Pope and Mother Teresa have us walking tall."

It was well after nightfall when we left the Convent of the Good Samaritan. Since the route to the subway is through dark warrens of narrow streets, Sister Julian walked the half mile with us to make sure we found the way.

After seeing us off she had to return through those dark streets and she would do it without fear. So it is not just sales talk when a travel agency here promotes Japan as "the safest country in the world."

Father Noel Doyle wants to make sure I am well read on the religions of Japan. In the library, on the second floor of Columban Central House, he urges on me book after book.

Through his guidance I have come to realize that it is not a good idea to put into pigeonholes the various religions of Japan. The lines of demarcation have blurred through the years. An individual Japanese may feel affiliated with several religions all at the same time.

While there is no such thing as a "Japanese religion," there are certain things that the Japanese want in any religion, no matter what it is called. H. Byron Earhart says that six themes persist in Japanese religious history:

1. The closeness of man, gods, and nature.
2. The importance of family—loyalty to the living and reverence for the dead.
3. The significance of purification, rituals, and charms.
4. The unifying forces of local festivals and devotional cults.
5. The weaving of religion into every aspect of daily life.
6. The closeness of religion and nation, with all spiritual feeling somehow supporting the national heritage.

Through the years Shinto and Buddhism have taken turns as government favorites. In 1945 Shinto was disestablished; since then all religions are supposed to be equal in the eyes of the government. Christianity gained in status after 1945, perhaps because it was the dominant faith of the victor.

From Shinto the Japanese learned to stand in awe of nature, feeling a closeness to it that is admirable. It helps them bring a joyful embrace to life and accept death as a normal process of nature. Shinto is from the soil of Japan.

Buddhism is an import. It arrived by way of China and Korea. In the beginning Buddhism's dreary outlook was in dark contrast with Shinto's bright acceptance of life. The early Buddhist teaching that human beings are chained to an unending wheel of suffering gradually evolved into the belief that one can break this painful repetition of *karma* by leading a virtuous life and so attain *nirvana*, described as being "like the peaceful merging of a drop of water into the sea."

Buddhism became more international and, in time, embraced almost every religious concept. Any contradictions are accepted as alternate aspects of the same basic truths.

After living side-by-side for hundreds of years, Buddhism and Shinto began to merge. Temples and shrines often became joint institutions. Many local beliefs could no longer be identified as either Shinto or Buddhist, so blended were the characteristics of each.

Because of such religious eclecticism, rural homes often have both Shinto and Buddhist altars. Many people prefer *chuto-hanpa* (a little of this and a little of that), what scholars call *juso shinko* (multi-layered faith.)

Since Japanese blend aspects of different faiths, this country has a total of religious adherents in excess of its total population: of the 120 million Japanese there are supposed to be 98 million Shintoists, 88 million Buddhists and nearly a million Christians. A scholar explained: "The real quest is to find the seed at the bottom of your heart and bring forth a beautiful flower."

When Father Thomas Grogan, pastor of Oiso, dropped by the Columban Central House, we were not long in conversation before I saw that he is a great promoter of kindergartens. He feels that they help the Church make its presence felt in a community.

"While scarcely any of the children are from Christian families," he said, "the parents prefer Catholic kindergartens because they teach personal discipline, high moral values, and manners. Japanese so value those things that they have no objection if the classes have a religious orientation.

"The graduates of Catholic schools may never embrace our religion, but they will always feel good will toward it. Christianity is not a threatening mystery to them; they have seen it from the inside and have fond memories of that milieu."

Father Grogan is optimistic about the place of the Church in Japan. He feels that the position of Christianity has improved in the past thirty years and gives General MacArthur some credit for it.

"The new constitution that MacArthur established has more of a Christian philosophy than the old one which had a Buddhist outlook. The new constitution stresses the individual over the group.

"MacArthur may have been the only occupation leader who was ever

147

liked. The very thing the Americans criticized him for—his aloofness—was the one thing admired by the Japanese."

Father Grogan has great hope for the Church in Japan. "Not on the books. Not big figures for baptisms. Thirty years ago we got large numbers of disturbed people—large classes. Now they come in twos and threes. But they have thought about it for years and so are more substantial.

"The Church's attitude is better, too. I have had funerals and weddings for pagans. I would not have been permitted to do that thirty years ago. Yes, things are looking up."

May 10
Tuesday

At breakfast Father Michael Scully recalled that just before the 1964 Olympics in Tokyo a Columban had said: "They'll make a fine city of Tokyo yet." Father Scully had laughed at him: "Impossible! It's such a shambles of a city. They could never make it nice looking."

When riding through present-day Tokyo, Michael Scully sometimes admits to himself that his fellow Columban was right and he was wrong. He is impressed with the modern city of shopping arcades, new buildings, wide boulevards, and even traffic jams. He is also aware that Tokyo differs from many modern cities in that it is clean. Twenty-years ago it was not this way.

When Father Scully came to Japan in 1956 there was just one subway line in Tokyo. Streets were narrow and tram tracks ran down the middle of them with just one lane for automobiles on either side. Except for the Ginza there was not much by way of shopping centers. The Ginza was famous, but Father Scully could not see what it had to recommend it.

"Perhaps it was the bargains that were available in those early post-war days," he said. "I can't remember any attractive buildings. There was, of course, the old Imperial Hotel, famous for having survived the great Kanto earthquake in 1923. There were also the shrines and temples which had, and still have, a beauty of their own. But I can't name any buildings in Tokyo worth remembering."

Things changed fast when preparations started for the Olympics early in the 1960s. By the time the games began, four subways were in operation. Streets had been widened and repaved and most streetcar tracks had disappeared. Little stores and houses which had lined the old streets had been removed to widen the new streets. In back of the little stores bigger and more impressive buildings had already been built so that the pace of life never halted. On the contrary it accelerated.

Father Scully recalls: "When construction of subways was going on, miles and miles of road were surfaced with sheets of steel. Those sheets of steel could be easily removed to allow for the excavation of subway tunnels and underground construction. At the same time the overhead metropolitan expressway was built. So in one great operation the underground system, the ground-level streets, and the overhead expressway came into being.

"With the coming of the Olympics new hotels mushroomed all over the city. Since then the tempo of life has never slackened. They have made a fine city out of Tokyo!"

Father Scully also speaks with enthusiasm of another phenomenon of progress that occurred in the past twenty-five years—the reclaiming of land from Tokyo Bay. He remembers that in 1956 the train going down the Chiba peninsula ran along the bay. People came out from Toyko to pick seaweed and seashells. When the tide was out there was quite a distance from shore to water's edge, but when the tide was in the water came close to the roadway and the railroad tracks.

The Japanese began filling in Tokyo Bay in earnest in the late 1950s. On the sixteen-mile stretch that has been reclaimed from the sea stand oil refineries, glass factories, chemical factories, shipbuilding yards, electric power plants, and steel factories.

"So there has been a population explosion in Chiba," said Father Scully. New towns have sprung up on the reclaimed land and on land that was once waste scrub. By the way, the new Disneyland is in Chiba prefecture, just across the river from Tokyo; it is on land reclaimed from the sea. Here is also the East Kanto Expressway which runs between the old airport at Haneda and the new Tokyo International Airport at Narita. This is a six-lane expressway but unfortunately it is not a 'freeway.' The toll is pretty stiff."

All of this has caused a big change in the life of Chiba prefecture. The northern part which was once rural and little populated has become urbanized and crowded. Such demographic changes and those that come in the wake of industrial development, have brought about vast social changes.

"This has a special meaning to Columban missionaries," said Michael Scully." We work there side-by-side with priests from Tokyo Archdiocese. Chiba, once a conservative and closed society, has opened up to the realities

150

of the modern industrial world. The people of Chiba have a new consciousness. Once they lived in what was called the 'bread basket' of Tokyo and
the 'backyard of Tokyo.' Now they see Chiba as the 'front door' of Japan.''

While listening to Father Scully tell of such dazzling achievements you
can't help but feel that the Japanese have proven the strength of their moral
fiber. They accepted the blows of fate at the end of the war and rose above
vicissitude. You wonder that such an affirmative attitude comes from a nation where suicide is held honorable. A missionary would say that this is
another example of the subtlety and complexity of the world as God created it.

Golden Week—that festive period from the Emperor's Birthday to Children's Day—is now in the past, but the Japanese are still looking for something to do. You might say that they are caught in an epidemic of doing. A
restless lot, they feel the need to see and to be seen. They seem to work at
leisure as hard as they work at their jobs.

"Since the Japanese have a passion for work," said Father Flinn, "they
have a difficult time coping with leisure. Like Americans, they discovered
that meaningful leisure is sometimes as difficult to come by as meaningful
work.''

He observed that youth takes the new leisure for granted but that older
generations are incapable of doing that. Those middle-aged or over take the
attitude that the virtue of work is all that they know, for they never had
time to learn to swim with the tide of leisure. They have not learned to use
it in the way that a Japanese intellectual described: "Leisure is the opportunity for the human being to give expression to his individual faculties in
an age when social systematization robs him of his individuality."

In a survey forty-six percent of people wanted more time for rest and
recreation; twenty-five percent objected to more leisure because they have
no way of enjoying it.

Many parents, especially working mothers, want their children kept in
school six days a week. Some say that one day a week is enough time spent
looking after kids romping around the local playgrounds. Others observe
that their apartments are tiny, and there is no room in the neighborhood
for children to play; so keep them in school six days a week.

This is not so unfeeling as it sounds. Fewer than twenty percent of Japanese are on a five-day work week. About ninety-nine percent of American
workers are.

The Education Ministry agrees with the parents that students should be in school six days a week; they need that much time to prepare for the dreaded "examination hell" which they will have to face. Strangely enough the Ministry approves a five-day week for teachers.

The national passion for work comes more from group loyalty than from love of money or ambition. Team thinking, team working, and team relaxing make up a pattern of life.

While watching television is the number one leisure-time activity, the Japanese are also avid readers. The amount of material printed in that island nation each year is amazing when compared with the population figures.

A report on leisure activities lists mahjong as having fifteen million players in more than fifty thousand clubs. Pachinko, a loud slot-machine game played with large ball-bearings in crowded halls with rock music shattering the air, is a rage all across Japan.

More active bodies spend free time at baseball practice fields, heated swimming pools, golf practice ranges, and archery centers. Since Michiko San met the crown prince at tennis, and so became a princess, the sport has increased in popularity.

And golf! With bars and cabarets costing $150 per guest, many businessmen now entertain their prospective customers on golf courses at only $50 per guest. Since membership fees and ground charges are high, and courses crowded, many Japanese find it cheaper to fly to Korea for a long weekend of golf.

Sooner or later everyone seeking leisure confronts the sheer mass of Japan's millions. During July and August it seems as if all able bodies are crowding buses, trains, and planes, seeking a summer holiday. On long weekends it is usual for thirty million Japanese to be on the move. Bullet trains are loaded with three times their carrying capacity, and still leave long lines of disappointed travellers on the platforms. High speed expressways have cars bumper to bumper and door handle to door handle. Tokyo airports become impossible. Every resort is packed.

This is a tough country for relaxing.

I will always marvel at Father Kevin Flinn's extensive interests. When he heard that 2,400 children, between the ages of five and thirteen were gathering in a hall in Tokyo to give a concert of classical music, he became interested in the man behind the event. So he wrote a magazine article about Shinichi Suzuki, teacher of the violin.

Suzuki said that the seed for his teaching method was planted in 1921 when he went to Germany to study mathematics, philosophy, and art. At the age of twenty-four he found he was having a terrible time with the German language; his ear could not hear correctly and his vocal cords, jaw, and tongue seemed to rebel. How embarrassing it was to observe small children learning to express themselves clearly in a complex language while he had such difficulty.

Since music is a language, Suzuki reasoned, children should learn it the way they learn any other language. They speak long before they learn to read and so they ought to learn to play by ear and from memory before they start reading music.

Dr. Suzuki's theory evolved around three points: (1) Every child can be educated; (2) education begins at birth; (3) if there is love much can be accomplished.

A "musical ear" can be developed, he said, and he can prove it by experiment. If a recording of one piece of great music is played for a baby every day for six months the child will clearly memorize it.

Suzuki said that if he had been asked to bring up Beethoven and Mozart tone-deaf he could have done it. "If I had two babies listen to out-of-tune music every day, they would grow into tone-deaf children. Children who listen to off-key nursery songs grow up with an ability to sing out of tune."

According to the Suzuki method violin lessons should be given about once a week. Since mothers play an important part in teaching children to talk, they should attend the lessons too. They are expected to arrive a half-hour before the time for practice so that they children may listen in on other children's music. The mothers are not mute bystanders; they take notes, learn the tune, and absorb all instruction given by the teacher.

Since politeness is very important, parents must teach their children good manners, to bow and thank the teacher each time for the privilege of learning.

Few of the mothers know the violin, but since they are the strength behind the child's training, they concentrate their efforts on inculcating Physical Readiness, which includes a natural approach to the violin achieved through proper posture, finger and bowing exercises, and the correct position of the violin; Musical Readiness which comes from listening to records and doing rhythmic exercises; and Good Manners!

Young people in Japan, like those all over, have lost touch with tradition. Having been born since the Second World War, they are unfamiliar with the old ways. When asked, for instance, about the origins of the New Year customs they shrug and say, "It is a custom."

Unlike their parents they are ignorant of how things began and what they mean. They don't know that the New Year customs arose because at that time of year Japan is supposed to be visited by three gods—Shogatsu No Kami, To-No-Kami, and Kada Matsu.

Shogatsu No Kami, for example, is the god who snips one year from life and clears away all unpleasantness. Since the god comes only to houses that are clean, children polish their bikes, the postman washes his red motorcycle, and even dog kennels and bird cages are scrubbed. The year-end hot bath (*o-furo*) cleanses the outer man, and the payment of debts clears the financial slate.

As for To-No-Kami and Kada Matsu, I am as ignorant of those two gods as are the young of Japan.

Tourists miss some of the most interesting sights in Tokyo. For instance, the Tsukiji Central Fish Market, the largest of its kind in the world. Father Flinn quotes the statistics: Six million pounds of fish arrive here each day and fifty-five acres of fish cover the wharves . . . over half of Japan's protein intake comes from fish . . . nearly a million Japanese are engaged in the fishing industry—more than four hundred thousand fishing boats sail from Japanese ports.

Many of the fishing boats range far across the seas even though the long, narrow islands are surrounded by waters that hold their own abundance of fish. In the cold water mass to the north are herring, crab, cod, and salmon. In the warm waters of the south, mackerel, tuna, sardines, skiptail, yellowtail, albacore, and sea bream abound.

What might stop many tourists from visiting Tsukiji Market is that they will have to get up at about 4:30 in the morning. The streets of Tokyo will not be busy at that hour, and yet the taxi driver might ask his passengers to walk the last few blocks because he does not want to get tangled in the congestion of the market.

In the twilight of morning, silver sheets seem spread over the wharves. These are silver-gray tuna neatly laid out row upon row. Swarms of fireflies seem to dart about, but they are really flashlights of inspectors and market agents. These buyers literally attack the fish. They probe with deep spikes to make sure that crushed ice was imbedded in every crevice. They taste samples and jot down numbers and weights. All in silence.

At 5:30 an electric bell gives warning. The quiet market bursts into hurried activity. The auctions are about to begin. Oven fifteen hundred fish handlers and buyers hurry in all directions. In groups of thirty or forty they mount wooden stands in front of the auctioneer and his two assistants. He chants strange sounds, incomprehensible to a tourist. A flurry of hands and a flutter of fingers signal agreements.

As soon as one section finishes a clamor of bells gives notice that other lots of fish are up for sale. As many as twenty auctions go on at the same time. The sounds coming from deep down in the auctioneers' throats are not exactly human.

When noise and activity subside brokers dart about among the fish placing the large, printed name cards on their purchases. This sets into action teams of men who have been standing on the side with two-wheeled carts waiting to carry off their firms' purchases. Collisions and traffic jams occur as carts weave in and out among the fish and the crowd.

At 6:30 the auction ends. In less than an hour several million dollars worth of fish have been sold. At this time 57,000 retailers, shopkeepers, purchasing agents and restaurant owners crowd into the market. Between 7 and 10 o'clock they mill around the 1,200 stalls and make the best deals they can.

The fish market evokes nostalgia in Father Flinn. Such sights and smells awake in him memories of the fishing fleets of the Caputos, the DeGenarios, and the Paperilos which were part of his boyhood in Port Pirie, Australia.

Another market, far more unusual than a fish market, should fascinate tourists in Tokyo, and yet few ever go there. Again they must get up well before dawn on a summer morning.

Fathers Patrick Diamond and Leo Baker both old Japan hands were so struck by the unusualness of the market that Father Diamond wrote an article about it and Father Baker provided photos.

The bidders are mainly children. Some arrive with their parents at a pre-dawn hour, but many come alone. They are there to buy insects.

"With more and more buildings going up in Tokyo," said Father Diamond, "almost every inch of ground seems to be covered with concrete. This and the high density of exhaust fumes make the sight of an insect rare.

"And yet it has been the custom of teachers to give primary school children a summer holiday homework assignment of collecting as many different kinds of insects as possible as a science project.

"You might think that with insects so rare in the city the teachers would relent and think of some other project. But custom is a powerful force in Japan."

The auctioneer announces the features of a larger than usual beetle—its exact length in millimeters, its weight and other characteristics. Brisk bid-

155

ding starts. Children prod and tug at their mothers to make them not give up, especially if a classmate is topping the bid. On some rare insects the price has been known to go as high as $500.

Some farmers, hearing the astronomical prices, wonder if they ought not quit tilling the soil and go chasing insects. Their wives tend to take the attitude, "What will the neighbors think?"

Country children provide most of the insects. They save enough of their earnings for a trip to the big city of Tokyo.

Father Diamond concludes, "There, in that vast city of over 12,000,000 people, they walk through a jungle of concrete buildings. A strange environment. No cricket chirps and no bird sings. Even a fly finds it difficult to survive."

While Tokyo has many interesting things happening within its sprawling confines, I do not find it attractive. Like Los Angeles it lacks a soul. Both reflect the spirit of materialism. Contrast this with a medieval town, built around a cathedral, where you can still walk with pleasure.

May 11
Wednesday

This last day dawns lovely, as has every day of this trip. April and May are Japan at its best.

I made a point of avoiding *tsuyu*, the rainy season, from mid-June until mid-July. The sunless drizzle makes for the most disagreeable time of year. Furniture becomes clammy; food spoils; shoes take on a green mould; and matches refuse to ignite. Traveling in a train is like taking a steam bath. Hospital patients suffer relapses. Suicides and murders increase.

Although *tsuyu* is a season of low spirits, there is a good side to it: Heat and moisture make rice grow.

Maybe I am wrong in telling the story of the Columbans while experiencing only the spring. It might lead to romanticizing their lives. Maybe I should have experienced the low spirits of *tsuyu*, and even come to know the penetrating cold of winter.

As the Japanese say, Ah so!

When we went out of the front door of Columban Central House, where rows of straw slippers stand in alignment, Fathers Scully, Doyle, and Vale and the housekeepers, Miss Atsuko and Miss Toshiko were gathered to wave goodbye.

Father Flinn, usually well collected on such occasions, became so distracted by all that *sayonara* that he started to enter the taxi wearing straw slippers, and would have managed to had not one of the housekeepers noticed.

It is a matter of face to have lots of people on hand when you depart or arrive in Japan. As we traveled around the country we saw relatives and friends galore waving and bowing *sayonara* to departing travelers. Company presidents are seen off by droves of office workers. Yes, it is important to have a good showing at the station. Saying hello and goodbye is an art in Japan.

At the terminal where I boarded the bus for Narita, a sign reminded me once again of how sensitive (and practical) are the Japanese about every aspect of life. The sign, posted on the desk where tickets are sold, reads: "It takes about seventy minutes to Narita airport, please go to the restroom beforehand."

Just before saying goodbye to Father Flinn I tried to tell him what a remarkable companion he had been during the past weeks, but as on most such occasions only inanities are mumbled. I wanted to say that he had helped me "see" with his more practiced eyes, and he did it without being indulgent. He gave me an experience that I will value even after impressions fade.

Finally, I stepped onto an escalator that took me upward toward the bus; he stepped on one that took him downward to the taxi rank. The last thing I saw of him was his grin, the one that suggests that he has looked upon life and found it amusing.

Every day on this journey I have thought about the troubled Year of Our Lord 1945 when the Japanese stood up in the ruins and went to work. They showed spiritual strength by knowing how to face a dark fate. Instead of shouting and filling the air with clenched fists and empty slogans, they rolled up their sleeves. They knew that affluence comes from toil, sweat, and self-sacrifice, and saw the direct connection between effort and income. So instead of letting suffering demean them they turned it into a victory of sorts. A less spiritual people might have used disaster as an excuse to drift from day to day, asking the world to feel sorry for them.

They put the war so thoroughly behind themselves that recently a Japanese school girl asked, "Pearl Harbor? What is this Pearl Harbor you speak about?"

The personal discipline of the Japanese is the thing that struck me most favorably. I found it in every part of the country.

Courtesy, a mark of personal discipline, shows especially in the quality of service. Taxi drivers, shop girls, waiters, and all others who serve us seem pleased that we are here. Such civility is not offered in the expectation of a better tip, for tipping is not done in Japan.

On my first trip here I made the mistake of leaving a tip in a small tea-room. The waitress pursued me nearly two blocks down the street to return it. She gave me quite a talking to, which I could not understand. Someone said she was probably telling me that one ought not be tipped for performing a kindness and that it is disagreeable to be reminded that one does things for others for the sake of money.

Such civility so delighted Isamu Noguchi, a Japanese-American sculptor, that he visits here often. He finds that even in humble pursuits there is love.

"It would seem to me," Noguchi said, "a maidservant in a Japanese inn or a Japanese farmer do their work more willingly because they take pride in what they are doing, not just because they are paid to do the work."

Each locality has its own traditional products and special dishes and people take pride in their specialties. This is true particularly in the country.

Artisans have pride in their work and love it, and so earning money is not their only objective. Evidence of this virtue is reflected in the many superb tools developed here long ago and still being made.

Noguchi said: "Traditional tools of Japan are superior to those of European origin. Here the craftsman and his tools are in complete unity. Where else is there such a profusion of useful tools? I was astonished when I went to a shop in Kyoto to buy a trowel and found thirty varieties. Abroad there would be perhaps five.

"In the United States where everything is mass-produced the types of hand tools become fewer and fewer. Machine tools proliferate. There is no question, though, that the best work is still done by tools which are an extension of the human hand."

Personal discipline is also indicated in Japan's literacy, about ninety-eight percent of the population is literate. My guess is that Japan takes education more seriously than any other country in the world.

The belief that knowledge is more important than money begins in the home. From parents and children the attitude goes out to teachers and to society as a whole. The Japanese bring to mind the immigrant parents in the United States and how they used to drum into their children's heads, "Get a good education! Nobody can take that from you. Money you can lose, but a good education stays with you."

Many of those immigrant parents were illiterate, but their children went on to become distinguished professionals and made America the world's leader. That attitude, more than advanced technology, is helping the Japanese get ahead today.

A visitor notices the interest in education in many ways. On the bus the driver may turn the radio to something educational, say to a lecture on children's health care rather than to rock music.

Educational television thrives. Language courses—English, German, Chinese, French, and Russian—are regularly scheduled. Courses directed at special groups, such as farmers or computer operators, enjoy a sizable audience.

Education never ceases. A man on the job is expected to keep learning. Housewives are taught how to do their work better. Adult education courses are filled. The four million Japanese who travel abroad each year see the trip as a chance to learn new things. The number of new books published in Japan each year, 32,000, is about the same as in the United States, and the circulation of Japanese newspapers, 67,000,000 is the same as that in the States, where the population is almost twice as large.

The Japanese are hungry to know.

Personal discipline is also reflected in the low crime rate. Of course it is no longer so low as when Lafcadio Hearn wrote about Japan early this century, telling of having lived in districts where people left their doors open all night and no case of theft had occurred for hundreds of years.

Yet the crime rate is still low compared with that of Western countries. In 1980 there were 1.4 murders per 100,000 people as against 10.2 per 100,000 in the United States. The incidence of robbery is 1.9 compared with 234.5 in the United States.

An offender is apt to be caught. The police are effective, largely because their communities are behind them. Citizens show a readiness to call them and the speed of response to a call is remarkable.

The police box system is one of the things given credit for curtailing crime. In each neighborhood a one-room office, *koban*, helps the policemen stationed there become a part of the community. A police official in Tokyo said: "If ours is among the safest countries in the world, the police box is one of the reasons. The police have to be a part of the community or it would be impossible to make it a safe city."

The police know when they capture a criminal that they have not done so in vain. The offender will be punished under the law. Maybe that is because in Japan there is only one lawyer for every 10,000 citizens while in the United States there is one for every 400.

The civility that comes from discipline shows up in so many ways: No

160

matter how humble the restaurant you are apt to get a hot towel to cleanse your hands before the meal . . . Where noise might disturb residents, panels which absorb sound are placed along highways. . . . Even though the currency is unfamiliar to you don't worry about being short-changed or cheated . . . White gloves are evident all over Japan, worn by cab drivers, policemen, bus drivers, guards . . . Uniforms are a proper fit and worn with pride . . . Almost everyone looks clean and well-pressed . . . Litter is rare . . . I kept on the lookout for the condition of cars and saw only one crumpled fender, no rust spots, and only one in need of washing . . . We used a great deal of public transportation—bus, boat, train, subway—and never was any of them so much as a minute off schedule.

Perhaps the Japanese are so disciplined because they have lived on overcrowded islands for a long time. They have to adopt ways of doing things that will be best for the group and reduce the individual's disruption of the common good.

The Japanese are not slobs.

Japanese in high places fear that their country will soon suffer from what they call "advanced nation's disease." Their Oriental awareness of the nature of things makes them realize that nations, like the tide, ebb and flow. That their nation will eventually decline is suggested in a list of new problems.

The most serious might be that young people, reared in affluence, are starting to take for granted the things that their parents knew they had to work for. Students threaten their teachers, even pull knives on them. High school principals quarrel among themselves as to how to handle such juvenile delinquents. At graduation in 1983 police guarded more than ten percent of the junior high schools.

Japan's educational system has always rested on the notion of *dotoku* which promotes the values of filial piety, loyalty, and a regard for others. Call it respect, or courtesy. That *dotoku* is fading is suggested in a white paper issued by the Prime Minister's office which says of today's youth: "They are devoid of perseverance, are dependent on others, and are self-centered." Without *dotoku* education becomes a shambles and when education declines incompetence is not far behind.

Among the young, especially in cities, pride in work is fading. The pursuit of the yen threatens to displace pride in a task well done.

As Chesterton said: "Progress is the mother of problems." Now that Japan is humming along as the United States did in the 1950s, it may soon

161

face the revolts and the tumult of the 1960s, and the inept public education system of the 1980s.

Old people are also causing problems, but in a different way. Since Japan is getting very old very fast there is danger that the pension fund will become insolvent. The elderly of Japan still have a better life than those in most of the world, but the tradition of living out one's life in the bosom of the family is a thing of the past. Much of the story can be told in a single statistic: a tiny Tokyo apartment costs at least $83,000, most are much more.

The perils of success endanger the Japanese way of life on other fronts. For instance, as the defeated enemy they enjoyed some sympathy, but now that they have become the nation with the second most powerful economy, they are on the receiving end of resentment. Something like annoyance faces them for having made peace pay.

Anger against the Japanese flares out in various parts of the world. (In West Virginia a charity raised money by selling sledgehammer blows on a Toyota.) The Japanese say that they are being set up as scapegoats, that they are blamed for American's sloppy business practices and its inefficient labor.

Akio Morita, the cofounder of Sony, a corporation that does three billion dollars in sales each year, wonders whatever happened to the spirit that did such an admirable job in developing America. He said: "You have such a spirit in your heart, but now you have forgotten it. Basically, Americans have the power and the courage. America was strong just a few years ago."

Akio Morita must feel uneasy when he reads the government white paper that says that Japan's youth are losing their moral strength. And he must cringe at the rise in nationalism that keeps repeating Japan is Number One in everything.

Such arrogance leads to *hubris*, the pride that precedes the fall. To predict Japan's fall is no great prophecy. All cultures and civilizations are as sure to disappear as the dinosaur, Pax Romana, and the carrier pigeon. The only questions are: How and when?

Throughout this trip I have marveled at the swiftness of change. Emotions have turned topsy-turvy since those days when Japan, Germany, and Italy were on our list of enemies and Russia and China were called friends.

I was also struck by the way the missionaries, too, have changed. As the missionary lightens his burden of dogmas he comes to appreciate the exhilaration of wonder and mystery. He gets rid of the us-against-them attitude. He learns humility by not having things go his way too readily.

162

Father Bede Cleary said: "Christ's admonition was 'Go ye into the whole world and preach the gospel to every creature.' Not convert, but preach. Make the approach. God in his time will give the increase when He wants it. One thing for sure, a missionary in Japan won't suffer from pride."

The airport lounge is filled with passengers who appear to be Japanese businessmen on their way to various parts of the earth to make deals and to see what they can learn from others. They are willing to learn, and will go anywhere looking for better ways to do things. They have been returning home, in recent years, feeling that their ways are better than what they saw around the world.

The Japanese not only built modern plants out of the rubble but have continued to keep them modern. A ten-year-old plant in Japan is obsolete. New inventions and new ways make it advisable to replace buildings and equipment every few years. That is why building crews work all night and all day.

Those of us over fifty can remember when the Japanese had a reputation for making junky goods. No one wanted to give a gift with Made in Japan stamped on it; so one Japanese town changed its name to Usa and stamped Made in USA on all its products.

During the war, I did a brief stint at teaching how to use captured enemy weapons. Pieces of equipment from Germany were substantial beyond their needs; those from Japan were so shabby they did not look as though they would last the morning.

When the Japanese began turning out products of quality they were called first-rate copycats. Now they are innovators. They have beaten the Swiss at watches, the Germans at cameras and at beer, and the Americans at automobiles and radios. The computer race is now on.

Japan has been more interested in producing engineers than in producing research scientists. Perhaps because technical improvement means an immediate payoff while basic discoveries may require years before a way is found for them to bring in dividends.

Therefore, manufacturers are fearful that their scientists will not keep up with the world in fundamental research. Some intellectuals believe that the Japanese are incapable of keeping up in the basics.

Some blame Buddhism for the nation's poor record in great scientific breakthroughs. The argument goes that the Judeo-Christian ethic makes clear-cut distinctions between good and evil, while Buddhism teaches that everything in the world is interconnected. So the Western mind is prepared from birth for the confrontational arguments and explicit statements of good scientific debate, while the Buddhists prefer ideas with fuzzy edges.

The spirit of Zen and the spirit of the Japanese language may both be getting in the way of scientific thought. A scholar said: "One reason for Zen's sustained success in Japan is its contempt for purely intellectual solutions." Another described the language as a "tongue full of allusion, suggestion, mood, and association of endless poetic nuance and possibility, which is the despair of abstract thinkers and the logical positivists of our world."

Other intellectuals complain that the stress on rote learning in schools retards creative thinking. They point out that Kyoto university produces more creative alumni than Tokyo university because it encourages more openness in thought and research. Of Japan's four Nobel prizewinners, three are from Kyoto and one from Tokyo. From Tokyo come political leaders and captains of industry.

The Japanese, in spite of dire predictions, are so determined to have all kinds of breakthroughs that they have well-defined long-range plans. Their Science and Technology Agency has recently published the official timetable:

The Japanese will conquer cancer by 2001.

There will be homes with three-dimensional television by 1997.

Animals and plants will be bred through cell-nuclei fusion by 1998.

There will be a month's advance notice on big earthquakes by 2006.

Hydrogen-powered cars will run on Japan's highways and solar power plants will be operating in space by 2008.

Japan will have a practical method for managing low-level radioactive waste by 1994 and of handling high-level waste by 1995.

This country will be building science engineering labs in space in 1995.

While inspiration cannot be willed, if you work hard enough it might come. Really caring, really wanting, are powerful subterranean forces that can gather and grow and finally explode into inspiration. Anyway, Japan should be the most interesting country in the world to watch during the next quarter century.

Pan American flight 12 left Narita and circled southwestward toward Tokyo Bay. Three rivers empty into the bay through courtesy of melted snows from the Chichibu mountains. All carry sediment and the waste of civilization so that the city grows southward as alluvial deposits fill in.

The chaotic view from above is not exactly that of old storybook Japan.

Yet it is full of reminders for anyone who knows the history of the country:

Into the bay Admiral Matthew Perry brought four ships, in 1853, to seek, at the point of a cannon, a treaty with the shogunate. The following spring he returned with nine ships carrying two thousand men. His gifts included Noah Webster's dictionary, a four-volume set of Audubon's *Birds of America*, and a hundred gallons of whisky. For entertainment he brought a blackface minstrel show. This time he concluded a treaty that opened to the world a Japan that had been secluded for centuries.

General U.S. Grant arrived in the bay aboard the warship *Richmond* in 1897. He gave some good advice to the Emperor Meiji: "Take the best of Western civilization and leave the rest."

General MacArthur, on the battleship *Missouri*, met in the bay with the Japanese Foreign Minister and the Chief of Staff of Japan's Army, who signed documents, dated September 2, 1945, admitting Japan's total defeat and so ending the Second World War. (The Japanese do not say that they surrendered in 1945; they say that they "terminated the war.")

The ashes of General Tojo, wartime prime minister, were scattered in the bay after he was hanged for war crimes.

Something about Tokyo Bay, said Kazuo Nishida, a journalist, evokes lines from the classic, *The Tale of the Heike*:

> In the tolling of the bell of the Gion Temple
> sounds the transitory nature of all things.
> The pallid color of the flowers
> expresses the truth that the prosperous must fall,
> that the proud do not endure for long,
> but must fade away like a spring night's dream.
> And like dust before the wind the mighty, too,
> will inevitably perish from the earth.